THE BALLAD OF TOM DULA

The Documented Story Behind the Murder of Laura Foster and the Trials and Execution of Tom Dula

By

John Foster West

Moore Publishing Company
Durham, North Carolina

ISBN 0-87716-019-8

For Dr. Arthur Palmer Hudson,

who taught me the meaning of my folk heritage.

ACKNOWLEDGMENTS

My warmest thanks are expressed to the following for their assistance in securing information for this book: The Honorable J. Luke Grayson, Mountain City, Tennessee; Dr. Louis H. Manarin, editor, North Carolina Roster Project, State Department of Archives and History; Dr. H. G. Jones, Director of the (N.C.) State Department of Archives and History; Mrs. Gladys Bracy, Research Technician, Tennessee State Library and Archives; Dr. John L. Bell, Jr., Department of History, Western Carolina University; Prof. J. Jay Anderson of Wilkes Community College; and special thanks to George Stevenson, former library assistant in the North Carolina Collection at Chapel Hill, without whose careful research this book would have been incomplete. Thanks is also due Mrs. Charlotte Ross, director of the Appalachian Collection at Appalachian State University and to Bill Smith, graduate assistant at ASU, for assisting in proof-reading.

PUBLISHER'S NOTE

It was long ago when I first heard the melancholic lyrics about Tom Dula, first heard the plaintive sounds of an old guitar as they caressed the words.

Growing older and coming to appreciate the beauty and gentleness of women, I began to have a special feeling for Laura Foster. She had to be lovely and pure and trusting. She deserved to be immortalized by song, remembered as another Juliet, Mona Lisa or still another beauty whose gentile spirit was gone but never lost.

John Foster West burst that illusion with his pen.

Growing up in mountain traditions, he writes knowingly about the times and places in which the Dulas and Fosters lived. His first book, TIME WAS (Random House), reveals his understanding of the region and his compassion for his people.

In this book, John Foster West analyzes a legend as thoroughly as one can from a century away. Although time erodes memory, certain truths come out of his many efforts and they are carefully reconstructed.

Now, without illusion, I share the author's pride in presenting this excellent contribution to the study of folklore.

Eugene V. Grace, M. D.
Publisher

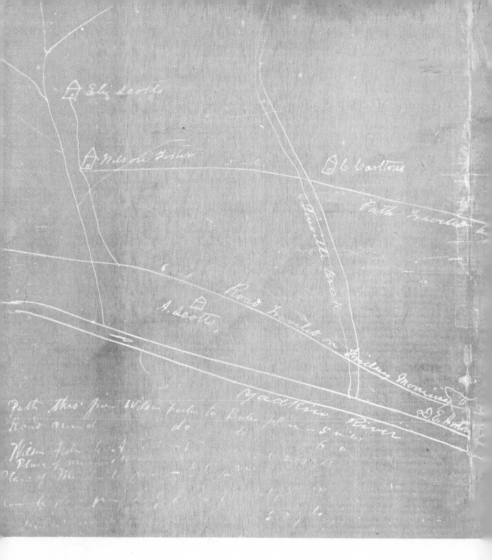

(Verbatim information in faint inscription above)

Path thro from Wilson Foster's to Bates place . . . . .5 mi.
Road around . . ." . . . . . ." . . . ." . ." . . . ." . . . . 6 mi.
Wilson Foster to A. Scott . . . . 1 mi.
Place of murder to where rope was found . . . . 100 yds.
Place of murder to grave . . . . 1/2 to 3/4 mi.
Grave to path from Lotty Foster's ' . . . . .150-174 yds.
Dula House to grave . . . . 400-500 yds.
Lotty Foster's to Mrs. Dula . . . . 1/2 mi.
From where rope was found in the bushes to
    the Stony Fork road . . . . .75 yds.

A Map made by

Col. Isbel [I] , and used on the trial

R. P. Buxton

I saw him afterwards that day passing along
On the next day Friday after breakfast awhile I
saw him coming from towards James Melton's &
going towards home. I again saw him going
back towards James Melton's; he was on the Stony
fork road, before the turning off place to the Bates
place. This was on Friday also. I saw him again
on the same day, about sun down going in the same
direction. A quarter an hour after he passed
this last time, I got a horse & went to James —
Melton's. Dula was not there. Ann Melton was.
I stayed there until midnight.

Cross Examined. A person on horse could
go to either James Melton's, ?
or to the Bates place.

Dr Carter testified. About the last of March
or first of April last the prisoner applied to me
for medical treatment. He had the Siphlis—
told me he caught it from Laura Foster.
The latter part of August or first of September
upon a ridge in 1/2 or 3/4 of a mile of Lotty Foster's
house in Wilkes County. I saw and examined
the dead body of a female, at the spot where
it was found. There being been a place cut
through her clothes & taking off the clothes in a
corresponding position on the left breast there
was a cut through into the body between the 3 —

& 4th ribs. If the knife have gone straight in it
would have missed the heart, if the handle had
been slightly elevated the blade would have cut
the heart, The body was lying on right side face
up — the hole in which it lay was 2½ feet deep, very
narrow, & not long enough for the body the legs were
drawn up, Such a wound, supposing it not to
have penetrated the heart, not necessarily fatal
though of a dangerous character - if it had penetrated
the heart necessarily mortal. The body was in so
decomposed a condition, I did not ascertain whether
it had cut the heart or not, The clothing around
the breast was in a rotten condition. A bundle
of clothes was in the grave,

<u>R. D. Hall</u> testified that the prisoner one day
about the middle of May last, at my house, as
he was coming from preaching, said to me
that he was diseased, and he was going to put
them through, who diseased him. I replied,
Tom, I would not do that

<u>J. W. Winkler</u> testified, There was a general
search made for Laura Foster I search 7 or 8
days myself, One Sunday 4 weeks after his
disappearance the neighbors were all out, formed
a search line, like a line of battle — we searched in sight of the Dula House, never saw him
engaged in the search. We searched behind the

On motion this cause was continued upon the part of
the State; upon the affidavit of Wilson Foster for the
want of the testimony of James Simmons, Lucinda
Gordon & J M McGasen

The following is the affidavit to wit

State
vs   } Slander } Superior Court of Law & Equity
Thomas Dula &   Fall Term A D 1867
Ann Melton

Wilson Foster makith oath that the
State is not ready for the trial of this case for want
of the testimony of James W McGrison, James Simmons &
Lucinda Gordon. That the said James W McGrison
& James Simmons are ready & testimony is interest'd
in this case; that the materiality of Lucinda Gordon
as a witness was not known until at Wilkes Superior
Court & that a Subpoena was issued at once for
said Lucinda Gordon, but that said Lucinda is
unable to attend Court on account of sickness to wit
Typhoid Fever, as affiant is informed & believes. That
the said J W McGrison is a citizen of the state of
& is now attending the session of the Legislature of
Tennessee of which body he is a member at this
time as affiant is informed & believe

That all the said witness are material & necessary witness
to the State in the prosecution of this Case, and are absent
without his consent or procurement, & that the State can
not come safely to trial without their evidence and
he expects the State to have the benefit of their testimony at
the next term of this Court & this affidavit is not made
for delay

Subscribed & sworn to before }   his
This 16th Oct 1867   }   Wilson Foster
C S Simmons Clk   mark

Military photograph of Col. James W. M. Grayson, who captured Tom Dula at Pandora, about nine miles west of Mountain City, Tennessee, around July 10, 1866.

Governor Zebulon B. Vance, who defended Tom
Dula in his trials for the murder of Laura
Foster. This photograph was taken several
years after the last trial; Vance was only
36 years old at the time he defended Dula
in 1866.

THE BALLAD OF TOM DULA

THE PROBLEM

The problem one encounters in writing about the murder of Laura Foster and the two trials and the execution of Tom Dula is finding out what *really* happened and verifying it as much as possible from documents contemporary with the events. The truth will not be served by interviews with individuals whose grandfathers or great-grandfathers were there and knew all about the murder. Neither will it be served by reading current articles and references in books written by those who have interviewed third- and fourth-generation authorities on the tragedy. For every such authority one questions, he will hear a different version as to who really killed Laura Foster; what happened preceding, during, and following the murder; and how Tom Dula behaved as he bravely faced the noose. After the lapse of more than a century, discovering the truth is possible only by studying legal documents related to the case and by examining any contemporary newspaper articles extant. The folk ballad and its variants give little information; the long narrative poem reputedly written by Linville Land is mostly fiction; and the oral traditions are varied, erroneous, and contradictory.

One needs to bear in mind that the Laura Foster tragedy was of far more than local interest to those contemporary with it. At a time when the nation was in chaos immediately following the Civil War, one of the country's better newspapers (and a Yankee newspaper at that), the New York *Herald*, sent a reporter to Statesville to cover Tom Dula's execution and to write the story behind it. The reporter telegraphed three columns of copy to New York, and his paper saw fit to publish it uncut in the May 2, 1868, edition, the day following Tom's death by hanging. A story would have had to be of unusual national interest a century ago, when the telegraph was not long out of its infancy, to warrant the sending of a three-column story (nine to ten double-spaced, typewritten pages) by wire — yet few people today with any knowledge of the affair are aware of the widespread interest at the time of the murder and the trial. Despite this contemporary publicity, the murder and sordid circumstances surrounding it doubtlessly would have been forgotten decades ago if it had not been for the ballad, which has kept the story alive in local tradition as well as giving it national, even world-wide, vogue through the version recorded by the Kingston Trio for Capitol Records in the 1950's.

Renowned folklorist Frank Warner writes of this controversy with Capitol Records in the October-November, 1963, edition of *Sing Out*:

> *Frank Profitt's grandmother, Adeline Pardue, lived in Wilkes County, N. C., where she knew Tom Dula and Laurie Foster. The tragedy was very real to her, and the song-story was a part of her life which she passed on to her children, Wiley, Noah, and Nancy. When Frank heard his father, uncle, and aunt singing the ballad it was not some story*

of a faraway happening. It was a personal possession, a family keepsake. He says it was the first tune he ever learned to pick on the banjo. It was clearly one of his favorite possessions that he shared with us that summer of 1939.

Frank's favorite mountain ballad became our favorite. From 1939 to 1959 I used "Tom Dooley" in every lecture and program, telling the story of Tom — and of Frank Profitt — and singing my own modification of Frank's version, having taken the essence of the story and reduced it from six stanzas to four, and — over many years — having reshaped the melody line to fit my own feelings about the song. It was this precise version that I taught to Alan Lomax and which he included, minus the second stanza, in Folk Song, USA in 1947. It was this precise version, all four stanzas, that I sang in my Elektra album, EKL 3, in 1952, with Frank Profitt's story on the jacket notes. It was this precise version, minus the second stanza, that the Kingston Trio, several years later, recorded on their Capitol record. How they got the song is their story.

The rights of a collector have never been clarified. Someone who knows how should write a law.

Ludlow Music, Inc., who came to hold my interest and the Lomax interest in the song, went to bat with Capitol Records. This, eventually, was resolved by a compromise, giving Ludlow full rights to the song as of January 1, 1962 — after the horse was out of the barn. By arrangement with Ludlow, fifty percent of anything coming to me from the song goes to Frank Profitt. That's our story. All we can hope for is that some day there will be a revival.

Since the ballad of Tom Dula (of which there are several variants) has become a classic of folklore and since the authentic, documented story had never been written, I hoped it might be a contribution to folklore as well as to any general interest in the matter to settle the problem of truth once and for all, so far as evidence available could make this task possible.

My interest in the murder goes back to my childhood, when I acquired my own version of the story from my mother, Elvira Foster West, and my father, John Wilson West, whose father, John Witherspoon West, was a member of the parties searching for Laura Foster's grave (this grandfather died before I was born). The fact that I was born and lived the first ten years of my life a few hills and hollows east of the murder area also added to my interest. "Tom Dooley" was one of the earliest songs I sang in a family headed by a fiddle-playing singing teacher. Though I later forgot everything but the chorus, the story of Tom Dula and Laura Foster has nagged me all the days of my life. At one time I wrote a novel called *The Ballad of Tom Dooley*, but fortunately it was never published. I say *fortunately* because most of my information was taken from a local newspaper feature story which has since proved to be ninety percent pure fiction. At another time I wrote a poem called "Cousin Laura Foster," but have since disclaimed any kinship with the hapless girl after learning what she was truly like. There is a bit of irony in the fact that I have finally expanded the precious time and energy and expense of research to get the need to write the true story out of my system and on paper — after almost half a century of thinking about it.

THE BALLAD

From HENRY, Mellinger Edward, editor. FOLK-SONGS FROM THE SOUTHERN HIGHLANDS. New York: J.J. Augustin. 1938. pp. 325-326.

A

Obtained from Mrs. William Franklin, Crossnore, Avery County, North Carolina, July, 1930, who learned it from her brother, Edmund Malone Johnson.

1.   Oh, bow your head, Tom Dooley;
    Oh, bow your head and cry;
    You have killed poor Laury Foster
    And you know you're bound to die.

2.   You have killed poor Laury Foster;
    You know you have done wrong;
    You have killed poor Laury Foster,
    Your true love in your arms.

3. I take my banjo this evening;
   I pick it on my knee;
   This time tomorrow evening
   It will be of no use to me.

4. This day and one more;
   Oh, where do you reckon I be?
   This day and one more,
   And I'll be in eternity.

5. I had my trial at Wilkesboro;
   Oh, what do you reckon they done?
   They bound me over to Statesville
   And there where I'll be hung.

6. The limb being oak
   And the rope being strong —
   Oh, bow your head, Tom Dooley,
   For you know you are bound to hang.

7. O pappy, O pappy,
   What shall I do?
   I have lost all my money,
   And killed poor Laury too.

8. O mammy, O mammy,
   Oh, don't you weep, nor cry;
   I have killed poor Laury Foster
   And you know I am bound to die.

9. Oh, what my mammy told me
   Is about to come to pass:
   That drinking and the women
   Would be my ruin at last.

B

Obtained from Mr. C. L. Franklin, the son of Mrs. William Franklin. The four stanzas recalled by Mr. Franklin vary slightly from stanzas 1, 5, 7 and 9 of A, but 7 is put before 9 in B, becoming there 3 and 4 respectively.

1. Bow your head, Tom Dooley,
   Oh, bow your head and cry;
   You killed poor Laura Foster
   And you know you're bound to die.

2. They had my trial at Wilkesboro
   And what do you reckon they done?
   They bound me over to Statesville
   And that's where I'll be hung.

3. Mama, oh, dear Mama,
   Your words have come to pass:
   Drinking and the women
   Would be my ruin at last.

4. Oh, papa, dear papa,
   Oh, what can I do?
   I've lost all my money
   And killed poor Laura too.

82.

Tom Dooley

Words and melody adapted and arranged by
Frank Warner

Piano arrangement by
Charles and Ruth Seeger

Moderately fast

Hang down your head, Tom Doo-ley, Hang down your head, and cry, Hang down your head, Tom Doo-ley, Poor boy you're bound to die. I met her on the moun-tain, And there I tuck her life, I

met her on the moun-tain   And stobbed her with my   knife.

CHORUS:
Hang down your head, Tom Dooley,
Hang down your head and cry,
Hang down your head, Tom Dooley,
Poor boy, you're bound to die.

1. I met her on the mountain
   And there I tuck her life;
   I met her on the mountain
   And stobbed her with my knife.

   CHORUS:
   Hang down your head, Tom Dooley,
   Hang down your head and cry,
   Hang down your head, Tom Dooley,
   Poor boy, you're bound to die.

2. This time tomorrer,
   Reckon where I'll be?—
   If it hadn'-a been for Grayson
   I'd-a been in Tennessee.

   CHORUS:
   Hang down your head, Tom Dooley,
   Hang down your head and cry,
   Hang down your head, Tom Dooley,
   Poor boy, you're bound to die.

3. This time tomorrer,
   Reckon where I'll be?—
   In some lonesome valley
   A-hangin' on a white oak tree.

   CHORUS:
   Hang down your head, Tom Dooley,
   Hang down your head and cry,
   Hang down your head, Tom Dooley,
   Poor boy, you're bound to die.

From Brown's NORTH CAROLINA FOLKLORE.

NORTH CAROLINA FOLKLORE

THE MURDER OF LAURA FOSTER

A

'The Murder of Laura Foster.' Sung by Mrs. Myra Barnett Miller. Recorded probably at Lenoir, Caldwell county, in 1939, 1940, or 1941. There is considerable melodic similarity between this tune and the version of 'Francis Silver's Confession,' 301B, by the same singer. With reference to the statement about "a long address to several thousand persons" made by Thomas C. Dula, (II 705) cf. *The Waning of the Middle Ages* by J. Huizinga (London, 1927), p. 3.

479

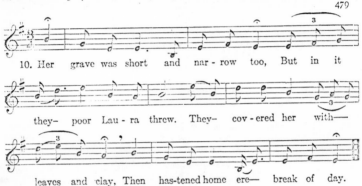

10. Her grave was short and nar-row too, But in it they— poor Lau-ra threw. They— cov-ered her with— leaves and clay, Then has-tened home ere— break of day.

Scale: Hexatonic (6), plagal. Tonal Center: e. Structure: abca¹ (2,2,2,2).

A(1)

'The Murder of Laura Foster.' Sung by H. McNeill. Recorded as MS score at Lenoir, Caldwell county, between 1921 and 1925.

480

The trag-e-dy I now re-late Is of poor Lau-ra Fos-ter's fate— How by a fick-le lov-er she Was hur-ried to e-ter-ni-ty.

Scale: Heptachordal, plagal. Tonal Center: d. Structure: abb¹a (2,2,2,2).

B

'The Murder of Laura Foster.' Sung by Mrs. A. I. Green. Recorded as MS score at Heaton, Avery county, in 1921.

481

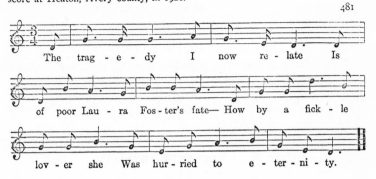

The trag - e - dy I now re - late Is of poor Lau - ra Fos - ter's fate— How by a fick - le lov - er she Was hur - ried to e - ter - ni - ty.

Scale: Mode III, plagal. Tonal Center: g. Structure: abca^1 (2,2,2,2). Circular tune (V).

TOM DULA

B

'Tom Dooley.' Sung by Mrs. R. A. Robinson. Recorded as MS score at Silverstone, Watauga county, in 1921. In the recording the sequence of the stanzas 1 and 2 (II 712) is reversed. This editor has an identical version of this ballad, which was sung to him by an old mountaineer ninety-five years old, who lived near Weaverville, Buncombe county. There are, however, some differences in the text. The phrase "Oh, hang your head and cry" can also be found in TNFS 73, 'The Lonesome Road'; also, "Bow down your head and cry" in CS 159.

482

2. You met her on the hill - side And there you may sup - pose You met her on the hill - side And there you hid her clothes. Oh hang your head, Tom Doo - ley, Oh hang your head and cry. You killed poor Lau - ra Fos - ter And now you're bound to die.

For melodic relationship cf. * FSUSA 300.

Scale: Mode III, plagal. Tonal Center: f. Structure: aa^{1}ba^1 (4,4,4,4) = Reprisenbar.

The following versions are from Brown's NORTH
CAROLINA FOLKLORE, II, 712-714. 1952.

303-A

A head note to this version indicates that it was submitted
by a Mrs. Sutton and that she described it as "a banjo tune"
and was composed by an old Negro named Charlie
Davenport, and sung to the tune of "Run, Nigger, Run, the
Patter Roller's After You."

1. Hang down your head, Tom Dula,
   Hang down your head and cry;
   You killed poor Laura Foster
   And now you're bound to die.

2. You met her on the hill-top,
   And God Almighty knows,
   You met her on the hill-top
   And there you hid her clothes.

3. You met her on the hill-top,
   You said she'd be your wife,
   You met her on the hill-top
   And there you took her life.

B

This version was "Sung by Mrs. R. A. Robinson, Silverstone,
N. C., 6/22/21." . . . from a song which has been sung and
played for many years (probably for over forty) in Watauga
. . . There is hardly a fiddler or banjo picker in our county
[Watauga] who cannot play 'Tom Dooley.' "

24

1. Oh hang your head, Tom Dooley,
   Oh hang your head [and?] cry.
   You killed poor Laura Foster
   And now you are bound to die.

2. You met her on the hillside
   And there you may suppose
   You met her on the hillside
   And there you hid her clothes.

3. You met her on the hillside
   Supposed to be your wife,
   You met her on the hillside
   And there you took her life.

C

This version from Mrs. Gertrude Allen Vaught, Oakboro, Stanly County, without date.

1. Hang your head, Tom Dooly,
   Hang your head and cry.
   You have killed poor Laura Foster
   And you know you are bound to die.

2. He dug the grave six feet long,
   And only three feet deep.
   He racked the dirt upon her,
   And packed it with his feet.

304-A

According to Mrs. Maude Minish Sutton of Lenoir, this version is "Dula's own song . . . His friends brought his banjo to him in Statesville and he composed and sang the ballad about his banjo and the murder."

1.   I pick up my banjo now,
       I pick it on my knee.
       This time tomorrow night
       It'll be no more use to me.

2.   The banjo's been my friend
       In days both dark and ill.
       A-layin' here in jail
       It's helped me time to kill.

3.   Poor Laura loved its tunes
       When sitting 'neath a tree;
       I'd play and sing to her,
       My head upon her knee.

4.   Poor Laura loved me well,
       She was both fond and true;
       How deep her love for me
       I never really knew.

5.   Her black curl on my heart,
       I'll meet my fatal doom,
       As swift as she met hers
       That dreadful evening's gloom.

6.   I've lived my life of sin,
       I've had a bit of fun.
       Come, Ann, kiss me goodby,
       My race is nearly run.

B

This version from "Mr. R. F. Greene, of Boone or the vicinity, in 1947."

One more night and one more day,
And where do you reckon I'll be?
Down in the valley, the valley so low,
Hanging on a white-oak tree.

From WELLMAN, Manly Wade. *Dead and Gone*. UNC Press,
1954.

Oh, bow your head, Tom Dula,
Oh, bow your head and cry;
You've killed poor Laura Foster
And you know you're bound to die.

I take my banjo this evening,
I pick it on my knee;
This time tomorrow evening
'Twill be no use to me.

I had my trial at Wilkesboro,
Oh, what do you reckon they done?
They bound me over to Statesville
And there's where I'll be hung.

Oh, pappy, oh, pappy,
What shall I do?
I have lost all my money
And killed poor Laura, too.

Oh, mammy, oh, mammy,
Bow your head and cry.
I've killed poor Laura Foster
And I know I'm bound to die.

Oh, what my mammy told me
Is about to come to pass;

That drinking and the women.
Would be my ruin at last.

This version of the Tom Dula ballad appears in a little booklet entitled TOM (DOOLEY) DULA, written by Thomas W. Ferguson of Ferguson and privately printed.

Tom Dooley

I take my banjo this evening
I take it on my knee
This time tomorrow evening
T'will be no use to me.

I met her on the mountain
Where I took her life
Met her on the mountain
Stabbed her with my knife

This time tomorrow
Reckon where I'll be
Hadn't been for Grayson
I'd been in Tennessee.

This time tomorrow
Reckon where I'll be
Down in some lonesome valley
Hanging from a white oak tree.

Walk up gents and ladies
Walk up to the stand
Walk up gents and ladies
And see Tom Dooley hanged.

I took her for my sweetheart
I took her for my wife
Then I took her around the hillside
And there I took her life.

I saw the wagon coming
To haul me to the tree
I saw my mother coming
To see the last of me.

Refrain

Hang down your head, Tom Dooley,
Hang down your head and cry
Hang down your head Tom Dooley
Poor boy you're bound to die.

Hang down your head Tom Dooley,
Hang down your head and cry
You killed poor Laura Foster
And now you're doomed to die.

Local version of the ballad which appeared in the Lenoir *News Topic* and in the booklet written by Mrs. Nancy Alexander, January 10, 1959.

TOM DOOLEY

I take my banjo this evening
I take it on my knee
This time tomorrow evening
T'will be no use to me.

I met her on the mountain
Then I took her life

Met her on the mountain
Stabbed her with my knife.

This time tomorrow
Reckon where I'll be
Hadn't been for Grayson
I'd been in Tennessee.

This time tomorrow
Reckon where I'll be
Down in some lonesome valley
Hanging from a white oak tree.

Refrain

Hang down your head, Tom Dooley,
Hang down your head and cry
Hang down your head, Tom Dooley,
Poor boy, you're bound to die.

Hang down your head, Tom Dooley,
Hang down your head and cry
You killed poor Laura Foster
And now you're doomed to die.

This variant of "Tom Dooley" was sung by Gray Temple, who learned it from his brother, Charles A. Temple of Charleston, S. C. It is played in E on guitar, also in A, and introduced by a long instrumental.

Poor old Tom Dooley, hang your head and cry.
Killed poor Laurie Foster, you know you're bound to die.

Took her on the mountain, as God Almighty knows,
Took her on the mountain and there you hid her clothes.

Took her by the roadside and begged to be excused.
Took her by the roadside, and there you hid her shoes.

Take down my old banjo, play it all you please
Come this time tomorrow, it'll be no use to me.

(Interspersed with initial chorus)

According to tradition, the following poem was written by Captain Thomas Land, a citizen of Happy Valley, soon after the murder. The events described are chiefly imaginary.

The Murder

The tragedy I now relate
Is of poor Laura Foster's fate;
How by a fickle lover she
Was hurried to eternity.

On Thursday morn at early dawn
To meet her groom she hastened on,
For soon she thought a bride to be
Which filled her heart with ecstasy.

Her youthful heart no sorrow knew
She fancied all mankind were true.
And thus she gaily passed along
Humming at times a favorite song.

Ere sun declined toward the west
She met her groom and his vile Guest;
In forest wild they three retreat
And look for Parson there to meet.

31

Soon night came on with darkness drear
Yet still poor Laura felt no fear.
She thought her lover kind and true
Believed that he'd protect her too.

Confidingly upon his breast
She laid her head to take some rest;
But soon poor Laura felt a smart,
A deadly dagger pierced her heart.

No shrieks were heard by neighbors round
Who were in the bed sleeping sound.
None heard the shrieks so loud and shrill,
Save those who did poor Laura kill.

The murder done they her conceal
And vow they'll never reveal
To dig the grave they now proceed
But in the darkness make no speed.

But dawn appears, the grave not done,
Back to their hiding place they run,
And there in silence wait till night
To put poor Laura out of sight.

The grave was short and narrow, too,
But in it they poor Laura threw,
And covered with some leaves and clay,
And hastened home at break of day.

The Search

Since Laura left at break of day
Two days and nights had passed away;
The parents now in sorrow wild
Set in search of their lost child.

In copse and glen, in wood and plain
They search for her but all in vain;
With aching hearts and pensive moans,
They call for her in mournful tones.

With sad forebodings for her fate
To friends her absence they relate,
With many friends all anxious, too,
Again their search they do renew.

They searched for her in swamps and bogs,
In creeks and caves, and hollow logs;
In copse, and glen, and bramble too;
But still no trace of her they view.

At last upon a ridge they found
Some blood all mingled with the ground.
The sight to all seemed very clear
That Laura had been murdered there.

Long for her grave they search in vain.
At length they meet to search again,
Where stately pines and ivies wave,
At last they found poor Laura's grave.

The Resurrection and Inquest

The grave was found as we have seen
Mid stately pines and ivies green.
The Coroner and Jury too,
Assembled this sad sight to view.

They take away the leaves and clay
Which from her lifeless body lay.
They from the grave her body take
And close examination make.

When soon the bloody wound they spied,
Twas where the deadly dagger pierced her side;
The inquest held, this hapless maid
Was then into her coffin laid.

The Jury made the verdict plain,
Which was, poor Laura had been slain;
Some ruthless fiend had struck the blow,
Which laid poor luckless Laura low.

Then in the church yard her they lay
No more to rise till judgment day
Then robed in white we trust she'd rise
To meet her Saviour in the skies.

By Thomas Land

DISCREPANCIES IN MODERN PUBLISHED VERSIONS
OF THE TOM DULA STORY

Many versions of the Tom Dula story have circulated orally over the last hundred years, and many others have appeared in print. In the twentieth century alone, one could safely guess that over 200 stories have appeared in magazines, books, newspapers, and in pamphlet form. It would be both futile and pointless to attempt to discover and record the many examples extant. Therefore, this chapter will discuss only nine written versions of the story behind "The Ballad of Tom Dula," along with one interview as representative of the oral tradition which has been handed down in the vicinity of Elkville.

These stories are as follows and are arranged and discussed in chronological order: "Tom Dooley," from *Folk-Song U.S.A.*, edited by Alan Lomax, 1947; variants of the story from Dr. Frank C. Brown's collection, *North Carolina Folklore* II (this volume edited by Dr. Arthur Palmer Hudson), 1952; "Bow Down Your Head, Tom Dula," a chapter from Manly Wade Wellman's *Dead and Gone*, 1954;

an episode from *The World of My Childhood* by Dr. Robert L. Isbell, 1955; *Tom (Dooley) Dula*, by Thomas W. Ferguson, 1958; "The Story of Tom Dooley," by Roy Thompson, in the Winston-Salem *Journal*, 1958; *Tom Dooley* by Nancy Alexander, 1959; an excerpt from *Land of Wilkes* by Judge Johnson J. Hayes, 1962; an excerpt from *Zeb Vance* by Glenn Tucker, 1965; and an interview with Wade Gilbert in July, 1969. "Tom Dula's Grave" and "More on Tom Dooley," by W. C. Burton, in the February 1 and February 8, 1959 issues of the Greensboro *Daily News*, were also examined, but since the two articles borrowed almost exclusively from Wellman's book, they were not included in this discussion.

Alan Lomax is among the more respected editors of American folk ballads; his version is a short introduction to the "Tom Dula" ballad which appeared in his collection. Dr. Frank C. Brown, a former Duke University professor, collected the material in *North Carolina Folklore* in seven volumes, one of the most complete and most respected studies of regional folklore in existence. Dr. Hudson, who was responsible for the versions of the story preceding the variants of the ballad in the Brown collection, is Kenan Professor Emeritus of English at the University of North Carolina; he is also one of the nation's most respected folklorists. Dr. Hudson is quoting those he interviewed and does not suggest that his versions are true. Manly Wade Wellman is a professional writer of both fiction and nonfiction, with some 50 books to his credit. *Dead and Gone* is a series of stories based on famous murder cases in North Carolina. Dr. Robert L. Isbell was a minister who was born and grew up in Happy Valley, near Elkville; *The World of My Childhood* is a short autobiography privately printed by the Lenoir *News Topic*. Thomas W. Ferguson is a gentleman farmer who was born near Elkville and still farms the land along the Yadkin River there; his version is a short pamphlet privately published, with illustrations drawn by his daughter. Roy Thompson was on the staff of the Winston-Salem *Journal* at the time his story was written. Mrs. Alexander was for many years a frequent contributor to the Lenoir *News Topic*; her version was in pamphlet format, although it originally ran in series in the *News Topic*. Judge Johnson J. Hayes was born and reared in Wilkes County near North Wilkesboro. He was United States District Judge for the Middle District (of N. C.) from 1927 until his retirement in 1957; his version is taken from his history of Wilkes County. *Zeb Vance* is a biography of North Carolina's Civil War governor; Glenn Tucker is a professional writer who has written several books dealing with historical subjects.

The most conspicuous discrepancy among the writers concerns the date of the murder, but that has been treated in a separate chapter. Next to it is possibly Tom Dula's war record: In what organization did Tom Dula fight during "the War for Southern Independence"? Obviously, the 26th North Carolina Regiment. Why? Because early in the war it was commanded by Colonel Zeb Vance; why else would this great man, ex-governor, come to the aid of Tom Dula, a nobody without money with which to pay his attorney? The apocryphal tales of Tom playing his fiddle and banjo around campfires for old Zeb naturally follow. It is impossible to determine where this error originated because it is stated as a fact in Lomax's version (he calls the 26th a calvary outfit), the earliest published, and he had it from Frank Warner, who was given the information by Frank Profitt in an interview. However, it is a common assumption in oral tradition, no doubt growing out of Vance's part in the trial.

Dr. Hudson does not mention Tom's regiment, nor does Dr. Isbell. But Wellman, Thompson, and Judge Hayes all state unequivocally that Tom fought in the 26th North Carolina Regiment. Ferguson, surprisingly, has Tom enlisting in the correct regiment (the N. C. 42nd) on the correct date and at the age indicated on his military record — *surprisingly* because his little book contains other errors common among the articles discussed. (Ferguson gives as Vance's reason for aiding Tom the "fact" that Jim Horton, a relative of Tom's, asked him to.) Tucker indicates that Vance went to Tom's aid because he was told by an unidentified person that Tom Dula had been a member of his old 26th Volunteers and was in trouble, but that Vance had learned later that Tom had been a member of the 42nd Regiment instead. Mrs. Alexander also has Tom enlisting in the correct regiment.

The "school teacher" myth is the most interesting one associated with the tragedy, adding romance to a morbid situation. It appears initially in the Lomax version and might have been borrowed from him by later writers and embellished by repetition. Lomax does not supply a name but states that a "Yankee" school teacher, who had been seeing Laura before Tom's return from the war, found the buried corpse and captured Tom later. No one else identifies the teacher as a Yankee. Wellman is the earliest of the writers to call him Bob Cummings, whom he describes as "small and lean." According to Wellman, there would have been no case against Tom Dula without Cummings, who (because of his unrequited love for Laura) led the posse into Tennessee to capture Tom, hired a laundress to spy on Ann Melton, and gathered the damning evidence against Tom, before turning it over to the prosecutor. Dr. Isbell does not mention either a school teacher or a Bob Cummings, but Ferguson does. He identifies Bob Cummings as the sheriff of Wilkes County, who went into Tennessee with Jack Adkins and Ben Ferguson to capture Tom. Thompson does not mention a teacher but states that the Grayson in the ballad was "actually Sheriff Jim Grayson of Wilkes." Mrs. Alexander's version is somewhat similar to Wellman's, except that she calls the school teacher Bob Grayson. She adds, however, that "some said his name was Cummings." Judge Hayes does not mention Grayson, Cummings, or a school teacher. But Tucker writes that a local school teacher named Bob Cummings, who had been rejected by Laura Foster, led a posse into Tennessee to capture Tom.

There is no Cummings recorded on the official list of witnesses paid by Wilkes County, and no school teacher is mentioned in the testimony. In fact there were no schools in the area during the Civil War and for several years afterwards, though this fact does not preclude the existence of an ex-school teacher. It is interesting to note how the name James W. M. Grayson became associated with an apocryphal school teacher and finally displaces the name of W. G. Hix, the sheriff of Wilkes County, through repeated borrowings of later versions of the Tom Dula story from earlier ones, and perhaps, from oral tradition.

Wellman describes Tom Dula as about six feet tall, good looking, in his early twenties, with dark eyes and curly hair. This is almost exactly the same description the New York *Herald* gave of Tom, undoubtedly the source of Wellman's information. It also closely agrees with the description on Tom's army record. However, Ferguson describes Tom as tall, with curly black hair and *blue* eyes. Wellman's Laura Foster was pretty, with chestnut hair and blue eyes — not quite the white, chestnut haired, dark-brown eyed girl Ferguson describes, nor the mousy, drab girl one of Thompson's sources depicts. (Tom Dula's description is well known, but there is nowhere extant a record of Laura's appearance. Oral tradition has her as somewhere between pretty and beautiful. Pauline Foster, in her testimony, simply describes her as having a gap between her front teeth. However, a native of Wilkes still keeps a lock of black hair, which she maintains belonged to Laura. Strangely, the above authors (excluding Ferguson), when they describe Ann Melton, the "villianess," at all, merely indicated that she was beautiful, although Wellman quotes the *Herald* reporter's enthusiastic panegyric to her great beauty and poise. Ferguson calls her a beautiful woman with a white complexion and black hair. Traditionally, Ann Melton was the personification of evil, and Laura was the good girl cruelly betrayed and murdered. Isbell calls Laura "a poor but respected girl." Ferguson says she was one of the best girls in the valley, a hard worker. Only Wellman agrees with the records, calling her "hot-blooded" and suggesting that she was promiscuous.

Although the date varies, most of the writers have the story correct concerning Laura's leaving home on a mare, except for small details. (Wellman calls the mare Betty; Ferguson describes her as a white mare named Belle; Mrs. Alexander and Tucker, a brown mare named Belle.) The Lomax version has Tom and Laura going for a walk together in the hills when she disappeared, and one of Dr. Hudson's sources states that the two, Tom and Laura, were on a horse together when "the other woman" stepped from behind a tree and stabbed Laura in the side.

After Laura Foster had disappeared, the mare was found, or she returned home by herself, depending on the version one reads. Wellman states that a man led the gaunt mare up to Cowels Store three weeks after she had disappeared, on June 10, saying that he had found her tied to a tree at the Bates Place. Dr. Isbell indicates that the mare was found two or three days after Laura's disappearance, tied to a tree just off Stony Fork Road, near where Laura was killed; and Ferguson says essentially the same thing. Mrs. Alexander is quite specific: On June 10, 1865, about three weeks after the date on which Laura actually left home, May 25. Since only Wellman is correct in this instance, it is very likely that Mrs. Alexander borrowed the correct month and day from him; however, her year is wrong.

The writers are in general agreement that a good many men, approximately 75, searched the hills for Laura Foster's body after the mare was found. As to how the grave was eventually discovered, they do not agree. Dr. Isbell's version tells how Ann and her cousin, Perline (Pauline) Foster, were arrested and how the latter turned "State's evidence" by taking authorities to a spot in a hollow where she had once waited while Ann Melton went on up the ridge to check on Laura's grave. The authorities had become suspicious after Ann and "Perline" had quarrelled at a party. Ferguson tells the same story: "Perline," Ann's and Laura's cousin, was at a party with Ann and quarrelled with her. In the heat of anger, "Perline" threatened to tell what she knew on Ann. "You'd better hush or I'll tell something," "Perline" threatened.

"You're as deep in the mud as I am in the mire," Ann is supposed to have retorted angrily.

Ferguson's order of events is not clear, but he implies that this is how authorities learned of the approximate location of the grave. Mrs. Alexander writes basically the same version: Two months after Laura disappeared, Ann and "Perline" quarrelled at a "gathering". After their heated exchange of words, suspicious authorities questioned them, and "Perline" took them to the spot in the hollow where she had gone with Ann (after Ann had told her that Tom killed Laura). It is informative to note that the exchange of words between Pauline and Ann, supposedly at a party in the versions above, corresponds to what actually happened in the fight between the two women at Mrs. James Scott's house, as revealed by the testimony in court; this is a classic example of how fact can become distorted in folk tradition.

The story of how the grave was actually discovered also has interesting variants. Lomax has his Yankee school teacher discover it one day while out walking in the hills, following a heavy rain. He catches a glimpse of Laura's scarlet cloak where some of the soil has been washed from the grave. Almost all the other versions include the incident of a horse snorting or shying after the animal smelled the corpse, leading to the discovery of the grave, and most of them identify the horseman as David Horton, as Col. James Isbell did in testimony during the trial. Wellman states merely that a horse snorted; Dr. Isbell, that David Horton's horse shied. Thompson's version has David Horton riding up a little trout stream called Reedy Branch, when his horse commenced rearing at some huckleberry bushes. Mrs. Alexander names six members of the search party: Col. James Isbell, David Horton, Bob Grayson (the mythical school teacher), Walter Winkler, Robert Kindall, and James Melton. David Horton's horse, she writes, shied from a certain spot, which led to discovery of the grave in an ivy thicket. Tucker varies slightly from the others in his account: He states that a rider detected a stench in an ivy thicket.

Eventually the grave was found, and everyone agrees that it was a shallow grave, approximately two feet deep, and too short for Laura's corpse. According to one of Dr. Hudson's sources, Laura's limbs had been broken so that her body would fit into the grave; another source told him that Laura was buried in a shallow grave, her head between her knees. Wellman writes that the corpse was doubled and twisted and that both legs had been broken. Dr. Isbell says that she was *crammed* into the short grave; Mrs. Alexander, that her legs were broken. These discrepancies are perhaps the indirect result of Dr. Carter's testimony in court that Laura Foster was buried in a shallow grave so short she had been turned on her side and her legs drawn up, so the corpse would fit. All of the writers were correct in their description of the wound, a knife stab in the left breast. Those who mentioned Laura's bundle of clothes, had it in the grave with her, either under or on top of her. Mrs. Alexander states that Laura's apron had been neatly folded into four folds and placed over her face.

Tom Dula fled the community immediately after or soon after Laura's body was discovered, depending on which writer is telling the story. Lomax, whose brief version is in a

Sir Walter Scott tradition, has Tom heading for Tennessee on a horse, while his brother led the posse off the track so that Tom could escape. The love-sick Yankee school teacher captured him, however, before he got out of the state. Actually, Tom owned no horse, and so far as can be determined from the records, his only two brothers were killed in the war. According to Wellman, Tom swore vengeance against the unknown murderer the day Laura's corpse was found, but by the next day he had fled from the area. Other young men had also disappeared — Jack Keaton, a former suitor of Laura's; Bob Cummings, the school teacher who had loved Laura in vain; Jack Adkins; and Ben Ferguson. Dr. Isbell writes simply that "Tom Dula fled the county and Ann Melton was in the Wilkesboro jail"; Ferguson, that Tom disappeared along with other young men of the community. The same succinct comment is made by Judge Hayes. Thompson does not tell when Tom left, but Mrs. Alexander's version is essentially the same as Wellman's and was probably borrowed from his, since she also speaks of Jack Keaton, a name which appears nowhere in the records, neither on the list of witnesses nor on the original justice of the peace warrant.

Both Wellman and Mrs. Alexander have essentially the same version of Tom Dula's capture and return. He and Jack Keaton (who was later released because of an alibi) were brought back to Cowels Store bound on horseback by Bob Cummings, Jack Adkins, and Ben Ferguson. Wellman gives the time as mid-July; Mrs. Alexander, as "on a hot day in July," three weeks after Laura's body was found (which is, incidentally, the same date she gives for the mare's return). Both writers include the story of the faked writ of extradition and how Tom, after his hands were unbound, played a gay tune on his fiddle for the onlookers at the store. (State governments in the South were in such a state of flux in 1866, it is doubtful that authorities would have worried much about the formality of such a writ.) Dr. Isbell has Tom captured in Virginia and returned to the Wilkesboro jail. Ferguson states that he was captured in Tennessee by "Sheriff Bob Cummings," assisted by Ben Ferguson and Jack Adkins. Thompson writes that it was Sheriff Jim Grayson who captured Tom, "some say in North Carolina, some say in Virginia, some say as far (away) as Tennessee." (Actually, Tennessee is somewhat closer to Elkville than Virginia.) Hayes states simply that "a group from Wilkes went to Tennessee and brought Tom back"; and Tucker, that a posse headed by local school teacher Bob Cummings went to Tennessee after Tom.

There are even discrepancies regarding the time (or times) of the trial (or trials), a simple enough matter for a writer to check. Most of the authors ignore the date of the first trial. Wellman gives it correctly as the fall term of Iredell Superior Court, 1866. But Dr. Isbell and Mrs. Alexander are far from correct. Dr. Isbell gives it as the spring term of Iredell Superior Court, 1866 (following the murder in 1865), and Mrs. Alexander, as the fall term of the same court, in 1865. Most surprising of all is Judge Hayes' date for the Grand Jury hearing, May term, 1866. (The hearing was actually in the fall of 1866, during the opening of the fall term of Wilkes County Superior Court.)

Some of the writers are vague about Tom's two trials and his appeal. Aside from the details concerning Bob Cummings' evidence, details which are not verified in any of the records, Wellman has the story pretty much as the *Herald* reporter wrote it. Vance's statement that he "had known Tom through strain and stress," could not, of course, have been true. But Wellman has the appeal and the second trial, in which he maintains that there was additional evidence presented against Tom Dula. (Actually, the evidence was essentially the same in both trials.) Dr. Isbell implies that only one trial was held. He states that Tom Dula was tried in the spring of 1866 and was hanged May 1 of the same year. He has Zeb Vance defending Tom Dula and Thomas Settle prosecuting him. (Although Settle and Vance were old political foes, Settle had nothing to do with the Dula trial.) Ferguson does not dwell on the trial, and all Thompson says is that Tom did not help himself when he took the witness stand. (Actually, Tom did not take the stand in his own defense.) Mrs. Alexander does not give a date for the first trial, but she implies it was the fall term of 1865 because, she writes, Tom was granted a new trial in January, 1866, as a result of Vance's appeal. Since Mrs. Alexander's date is two years off, as Dr. Isbell's is, it appears probably that her article borrowed from his — probably because both versions appeared originally in the Lenoir *News Topic*, his somewhat earlier than Mrs. Alexander's. In fact, Mrs. Alexander wrote a brief introduction to Dr. Isbell's book. They are the only two writers who have the murder occurring in 1865, the trial between then and spring of 1866, and the execution in 1866. Aside from the error regarding the date of the Grand Jury hearing, Judge Hayes is essentially correct in his treatment of the trial date, and Tucker does not mention it.

There are, naturally, different versions of Tom's behavior as he faced execution, some of them derived from the New York *Herald* account and some of them undoubtedly apocryphal. Lomax states that Tom Dooley himself "made up" the "Tom Dooley" ballad and sang it as he rode in a cart on the way to be hanged. Wellman writes that Tom was baptized the morning of the execution date, was taken from his cell before noon by Sheriff Wasson, and that he rode to the jibbet in a wagon and sat on the coffin prepared for him, playing on his fiddle. Tom addressed the throng of spectators for about an hour, according to Wellman, and joked about the rope that was to hang him: "You have such a nice, clean rope," he is said to have told the sheriff. "I ought to have washed my neck." According to Dr. Isbell, "As Tom stood on the platform, he raised his hand high above his head and said, 'Gentlemen, do you see this hand? Does it tremble? I never hurt a hair of the girl's head.' " Ferguson does not mention the execution scene, but Thompson gives two versions of Tom's words, one of them similar to Wellman's and the other: "Boys, stay clear of fiddlin', women and whiskey." Mrs. Alexander has about the same version as Wellman — the ride to the gallows fiddling "jaunty tunes" as he sat on his own coffin and joked with those who walked alongside the wagon. She states that the sheriff was W. E. *Watson*, rather than Wasson, to whom Tom made the remark about washing his neck because of the clean rope. Tucker also writes that Tom "rode atop his coffin and scraped his fiddle to amuse the trailing crowd."

All the stories agree as to the location of Tom Dula's grave, or what is accepted today as the location. Wellman writes that Tom was laid to rest near his home under an apple tree. Dr. Isbell states that he was "buried in the family graveyard by the side of the old Wilkesboro and Lenoir road, one mile below Elkville"; Mrs. Alexander gives pretty much the same version; Ferguson writes: "Tom was laid to rest near his old home underneath an apple tree"; Thompson: They buried Tom Dula "down toward the river from his house." Neither Judge Hayes nor Tucker mentions the grave.

Without exception, the writers who refer to the grave imply or state that it was near Tom Dula's home. Ferguson writes:

> Tom's house was a log cabin structure on a beautiful promentory overlooking the Valley. It was built about 1850 and was located in a profusion of honeysuckle and roses. The jagged shoals in the river's bed could be seen readily from the front veranda.

Here is an example of one of the errors in Ferguson's version and an error implicit in most of the others. Tom's home was nowhere near the traditional grave spot. A wealthy land owner lived in the area of the grave, a man named Bennett Dula, and Ferguson might very well be describing his old home. Whether Tom, who was poor hill folk, was even related to Bennett Dula is doubtful. But there are records to clearly indicate that Tom lived with his mother on Reedy Branch, near the Stony Fork Road, perhaps two miles from the grave spot. The proof is indisputable. It is clearly indicated on Colonel James Isbell's map, Exhibit A in the trial. For the same reason, Thompson's story of the bloody floor in the old Dula house is proved to be apocryphal. *Why* Tom Dula should have been buried on Bennett Dula's land or near his house (if he really was) is another matter.

The trial and demise of Ann Melton is interesting, as it is related by the various writers. Wellman, Dr. Isbell, and Judge Hayes indicate that Ann, defended by Vance, was tried during the fall term of Wilkes County Superior Court (Isbell, in 1866; Wellman and Hayes, in 1868) and acquitted. Ferguson states that Ann's attorney "won one delay after another," before her trial was held; and Mrs. Alexander, that Ann was freed "after several stays of sentence." Of course neither statement is true. Since Tom Dula and Ann Melton's original trial was "severed," Ann *could not* be tried until Tom's case was settled, and she spent two years waiting in the Statesville jail. She was tried during the fall term of Wilkes County Superior Court, 1868, probably the earliest date open following Tom's second trial and appeal.

As to when and how Ann Melton died, there is no information extant other than folklore, and one version is as dependable as another. One of Dr. Hudson's sources in *North Carolina Folklore* told him that Ann confessed to the murder on her death bed and that you could hear meat frying and see black cats running up and down the walls on the night she died. In Wellman's version, Ann was injured several years after her trial when a wagon in which she was riding overturned; the devil came to take her back to hell with him, while the sound of frying meat was heard and black cats climbed the wall. Ferguson states simply that Ann died several years after the tragedy, and that she confessed to her husband on her death bed, but he never disclosed the secret. Thompson writes that "some say Ann died of blood poison following child birth; others say an ox cart turned over and pinned her beneath it, and that she confessed to her husband on her death bed." Mrs. Alexander attributes her death to the overturned ox cart. Tucker says the same thing, and adds that the folk believed this was retribution from Satan.

The following version of the Tom Dula story is presented here verbatim because it is short and so different from the written ones discussed above. It was given to me by Wade Gilbert in an interview at his home near Ferguson in early July, 1969. Mr. Gilbert was then 81 years old.

Tom Dooley told Laurie Foster he would marry her. Laurie got on her daddy's horse and rode down the road to a place where she was killed. She met an old woman who had been a slave named Aunt Appline at Elk Creek and told her where she was going.

Ann Melton and Pawline Foster, her sister, held Laurie Foster, and Tom Dula stabbed her. They carried her body wrapped in a sheet and tied to a pole held between them down the ridge and buried her at night. They had to break her legs to fit her into the short grave.

Old man Foster's horse was gone several days. One day he found it eating in a field. It had been tied to a tree close to where Laurie was killed and broke loose. They found the tree where it had been tied. Folks started looking for the grave and finally found it. One day before Laurie was killed, Tom Dooley was eating dinner at Rufus and Nancy Hall's house, and Rufus went outside in the yard with Tom. Tom said, "If I live, I'll kill the woman who give me the disease, if it's the last thing I do on earth." Laurie Foster was a nice woman. I never heard nothing against her.

When that old Pawline Foster saw she was in trouble, she turned State's evidence against Tom and Ann Melton. Her mother rode a horse down the river road to Wilkesboro and raced with old man Foster to see who would get there first to turn State's evidence. Pawline's mother won. Grayson caught Tom Dula over in Tennessee, and he was brought back to stand trial.

Old Lott Foster, Ann Melton's mother, would get down in the floor dead drunk. Ann Melton would lay with just about anybody that come along. Sometimes she would do it with haulers who camped with their wagons not too far from her home for tobacco, cloth, or anything they had. She would lock her younguns up in the house by theirselves and leave them all night. She had two girls, but I don't know when they were borned. One was named Jane and the other one, Ida. Ida moved away to Caldwell (County), and I don't know what became of her. Jane married a good man and had nine children. They were good, decent folks.

After Ann Melton died, my grandmother, Lou Isa Gilbert, married James Melton. He was a good man.

The many discrepancies concerning the Tom Dula-Laura

Foster story existing in the above versions emphasize the problem one encounters when trying to separate fact from myth, even in published variations written by reputable authors, when the variations have depended ultimately on oral tradition for most of their "facts." It is obvious that some of the more recent articles borrowed from the earlier ones, but it is also apparent that the earlier ones depended significantly on interviews, especially regarding the more apocryphal aspects of the details. For example, as has been stated before, there is nowhere in the records anyone named Bob Cummings or Jack Keaton, not even on the list of witnesses, which is quite complete. If anyone had been as involved in the case as these two men are reported to have been in some of the stories, then surely they would have been subpoenoed to appear as witnesses. The school teacher, Yankee or otherwise, appears to be pure myth. Lomax has it indirectly from Frank Profitt's grandmother. This is in no way to impugn the veracity of these good people; it is an example of what folklore really is and how it develops. Our family version came from our father, told to him by his father, who helped search for Laura Foster's grave, and it contains a great deal of the same folk myth.

The important point to be made here is that "The Ballad of Tom Dula" and the myths surrounding it serve as classic examples showing how folklore grows up around most folk ballads and how the two complement each other. Discovering what really happened to Tom Dula and those involved in the tragedy clarifies the relationship of all folk ballads to the montage of facts and myths upon which they are based.

GEOGRAPHY

Beginning as a spring near the Green Park Hotel in Blowing Rock, the Yadkin River flows in a south-southeasterly direction down through the mountains and hills until it reaches Patterson, in Caldwell County, twenty miles from its source. There it takes an abrupt turn to the left and flows northeast, past Ferguson, Wilkesboro, and Elkin, turning eastward, then southward, farther along its course. The region between Patterson and Wilkesboro has been known as Happy Valley since early days. The community of Elkville, not quite half way between Patterson and Wilkesboro, is where Laura Foster was murdered in 1866.

Professor Elisha Mitchell [for whom Mt. Mitchell is named] says in his notes taken while on a geological exploration of the valley in the summer of 1828: "This upper valley to the Yadkin is delightful; from half a mile wide, bounded by ranges of mountains of moderate size, the Brushy Mountains on one side and a small chain parallel to the Blue Ridge on the other; the land is very fertile, pleasant to cultivate and produces immense quantities of corn; the air is salubrious and healthy and the soil occupied by very respectable farms." (*Echoes*, p. 5) In his *Happy Valley*, Hiekerson writes, "The bottom lands of this valley were luxuriantly rich for growing corn, wheat, melons, and vegetables." (p. 1)

Plantations began to spring up along the Yadkin River in Happy Valley as early as the 1780's. Reverend Isbell states that on the river east of Elk Creek, Benjamin Howard settled soon after marrying in Baltimore in 1762 and was there when Daniel Boone was a citizen of Beaver Creek, four miles down the river. At the close of the Revolutionary War a pioneer from Virginia, an ex-soldier named Captain William Dula, came into the valley. He became the outstanding land owner for many miles along the river, and his six children were located on prosperous plantations there. Another early settler was Thomas Isbell, great-grandfather of the author. At the time of the Civil War and immediately afterward, the plantation owners in the immediate area were the Dulas, Hortons, Isbells, and Joneses, all direct descendants of the original settlers.

These were the aristocrats of Happy Valley who had very little to do with the "pore white trash" living in the hills and on the ridges along the valley. These people lived in small pole cabins on patches of upland or along branches, on land owned by themselves, or on the outer fringes of some of the plantations. Reverend Isbell says that there were good people among them, but he speaks of them with condescension. Many of them and their descendants became tenant farmers on the large river farms after the end of slavery. Laura Foster's father and brother were at one time tenants on the land belonging to the author's uncle. Reverend Isbell writes: "It was an unheard of thing to invite the tenant class to take part in the socials of the land owners; however pretty the girls might be or handsome the men, custom barred their mingling together in social life." (p. 152) The same custom separated the aristocrats from the hill folk at the time of the murder.

The Fosters, the Dulas, the Meltons, the Scotts — all those involved in the murder of Laura Foster and the trial of Tom Dula — were from among the class living in the hills with the exception of several witnesses who were valley land owners. Whether Thomas C. Dula, the alleged murderer, was any relation to the Dula aristocrats is impossible to determine from records; indications are that he was not. *Foster* was also a common name among the landed gentry as well as among the hill folk.

From the article in the New York *Herald* comes this excerpt:

> *The community in the vicinity of this tragedy is divided into two entirely separate and distinct classes. The one occupying the fertile lands adjacent to the Yadkin river and its tributaries, is educated and intelligent, and the other, living on the spurs and ridges of the mountains, is ignorant, poor and depraved. A state of immorality unexampled in the history of any country exists among these people, and such a general system of freeloveism prevails that it is "a wise child that knows its father." . . . It is a poor country, covered with thickets and a dense undergrowth.*

Although a wide social gap between the hill and river dwellers existed, the Yankee reporter has exaggerated the social conditions among the hill folk. Anyone who has lived among these people will maintain that even though the depraved families did (and do) exist, living on the adjacent hillside or beyond the next ridge might be found the most industrious, honest, and moral family to be found anywhere.

"Elk Creek flows into the Yadkin River . . . after a

journey of twenty-five miles from its source on the Blue Ridge and of more than 3,000 feet above sea level," Reverend Isbell writes. "It is a turbulent stream and moves rapidly between the gorges and the foothills of the mountains through which it has made its way from time immemorial and is usually crystal clear." (p. 116) Calvin J. Cowles moved from Hamptonville in 1846 and established a store at the mouth of Elk Creek. He was the first man in Wilkes County to deal in roots and herbs. (*Happy Valley*, p. 53) A post office was also established at Cowles Store, which retained its name after Calvin moved to Wilkesboro in 1858.

This establishment was the heart of Elkville. Reverend Isbell writes that the store was the gathering place for all of Elk Creek, Stony Fork, and communities up and down the Yadkin River for miles in both directions. Most everything that came through the country in the way of shows and entertainment played at Elkville. Elkville, he continues, was located at a delightful spot on an upland slope overlooking the fertile valley "with large oaks standing around like sentinels to protect the peace and dignity of the place." Before Lenoir was born, Reverend Isbell writes, Elkville was a noted place and a muster ground for the militia. It was a place for public speaking during political campaigns, and great crowds came to hear the vital questions discussed. Laura Foster lived with her father in Caldwell County, west of Linville Creek; at an almost equal distance on the east side of Elkville, Tom Dula lived with his mother and sister beside Reedy Branch. Cowles Store was the community center, where a magistrate (Justice of the Peace) held local court and where the township deputy sheriff might be found when not at home.

Today, a combination service station-grocery store is the gathering place at Elkville, near where Cowles Store once stood. In the area of Reedy Branch, a mile and a half to the north-east across the hills, the old Stony Fork road is still there where it has been for over a century, somewhat wider than it was in Tom Dula's day and graveled. It leaves the Elk Creek Road about a half mile upstream from the river and turns north-east, following valleys and cutting across the spurs of ridges that run chiefly in a south-easterly direction, paralleling the branches and brooks which are meandering toward the Yadkin River. Reedy Branch flows through a tranquil green valley as bucolic and peaceful as one could find anywhere in the foothills.

You can stand in the road and see low green mountain ranges along the skyline in the near distance at either end of the valley. Where the Dulas and the Fosters and the Meltons once lived and eeked out an existence from the land, the people today live in comfortable modern houses or neat trailers and commute daily to Lenoir, where they work in one of the furniture factories. Rudolph Witherspoon lives with his family in a huge trailer where the Bates place is marked on Colonel Isbell's map. The spot where Laura was murdered is a few hundred yards away on the ridge above. The Turner Morley family lives on the spur of the ridge across the valley from Witherspoon in a trailer, close to the spot where Lotty Foster's house stood a century ago. Ann Melton is buried on the slope below his home. The old Reedy Branch road, which followed for decades the earlier path between Lotty Foster's house and Mary Dula's, down the branch a ways, is grown up in weeds and grass, snake country, Rudolph Witherspoon called it; but you can still recognize the bluff where Tom was seen "skelping" with Lottie's mattock the day before the murder. Banner Triplett's is the closest house to the grave spot, and is about half way between it and the Stony Fork road.

The trees in the area where the murder was committed and farther down Laura Foster Ridge, where she was buried, have been cut over so many times for lumber, the forest has been thinned out somewhat, though there is still a scattering of laurel and ivy thickets in the area of the grave. If Tom Dula could return today to the little valley, he would be amazed at the houses and automobiles along the old Stony Fork Road, but he would still feel comfortable in the woods where the tragic drama was enacted in 1866.

DATE OF MURDER

What Was the Date of Laura Foster's Murder?

The many contradictions in the folklore surrounding the murder of Laura Foster are understandable because folklore lives through oral traditions, and the exact truth seldom survives in this manner. It is easy to understand how articles written about such an event a century later can deviate from the facts, how they can be contradictory, since such articles depend on folk traditions, usually information from third- or fourth-generation "experts." What is not easy to understand is how legal documents with such a fatal bearing upon this murder case could be contradictory in such a simple matter as the date of the murder — or how a contemporary newspaper article could fall into the same error.

Yet that is exactly what happened concerning the date on which Laura Foster was murdered. In the Bill of Indictment (of Tom Dula and Ann Melton) presented to the Superior Court of Wilkes County during the fall term of 1866, the date of death is given as June 18, 1866 (a Monday). The

Solicitor's (prosecutor) opening statement to the Court at the fall term of Superior Court of Iredell County, opening Tom Dula's first trial, in 1866, gave the date of the murder as May 28, 1866 (a Monday). The first ruling written by the North Carolina Supreme Court gives the date only as May, 1866, and the second ruling, the date of Friday, January 25, 1866. Judge William M. Shipp, who presided at the second trial of Dula in January, 1868, indicates the date of death as Friday, May 25, 1866, in his report of the trial to the Supreme Court. And the article published in the New York *Herald*, reporting Tom Dula's execution, states that Laura Foster was killed on May 28, 1866.

In present-day accounts, the one written by Judge Johnson J. Hayes in *Land of Wilkes*, a history of Wilkes County, gives the date of death as January 25, 1866 (a Thursday). Reverend Isbell's date in *The World of My Childhood* is Spring, 1865, and Mrs. Alexander's article in the Lenoir *News-Topic* lists the date as May Day, 1865; apparently she means May 1, which was a Thursday.

The last two dates are so obviously in error, being the wrong year, they will not require further mention. But the discrepancies in the legal documents are amazing, to say the least: June 18, 1866; May 28, 1866; Friday, January 25, 1866 (the 25th was a Thursday); Friday, May 25, 1866. It is difficult to understand why the legal counsel for Dula, whose defense was otherwise brilliant, did not discover these contradictions and use them in the appeal. It is even more difficult to understand why the two judges who tried the case or why the state Supreme Court judges failed to discover such grave errors.

But the important task here is to try to determine what was the exact date of Laura Foster's murder and to support it if possible with evidence contemporary with the event, written evidence. Despite the confusion in the legal documents, this can be done beyond "reasonable doubt," and it can be verified from evidence presented at the trial.

These witnesses testified as follows concerning the date:
Betsy Scott — I saw Laura the Friday morning she disappeared.

Carl Carlton — I saw the prisoner on the Friday morning of Laura's disappearance.

Hezekiah Kindall: I saw the prisoner on that Friday morning about eight o'clock.

Mrs. James Scott — I saw the prisoner on that Friday morning after breakfast.

Pauline Foster — I saw the prisoner early that Friday morning at James Melton's house . . . I saw the prisoner on Thursday morning, the day before. Under cross examination: It was after breakfast on Friday some eight or nine o'clock [when she saw the prisoner].

Martha Gilbert — On Wednesday or Thursday before the Friday of Laura Foster's disappearance I saw the prisoner.

Thomas Foster — On Thursday before the Friday [of Laura's disappearance], etc.

Washington Anderson — I was at James Melton's on Thursday night before the Friday Laura Foster disappeared.

Mary Dula — Thomas was not at my house early in the morning of that Friday.

From this evidence, one must accept the fact that Laura Foster left home on a Friday morning and was murdered sometime that same day. The entire trial hinges on the fact that it was a Friday and that a good many witnesses remembered it was a Friday on which they had seen either Tom Dula or Laura Foster on the way to the Bates place, where the murder occurred. Only one of the dates cited in the legal documents falls on a Friday; that is May 25, 1866, in Judge Shipp's report.

The month of January as the season when the murder occurred can be ruled out rather easily. In her testimony, Pauline Foster stated that on the Friday morning Laura disappeared she (Pauline) "had started out to the field to plant corn." Further along in the trial she said that she "stayed in the field at work with Jonathan Gilbert and James Melton [whom she worked for] until three o'clock." And at another point she testified that she was "dropping corn," a method of planting used before the invention of the corn planter. (One worker would drop two or three grains of corn at close intervals in a furrow, and another worker would follow, covering the seed with a hoe.)

It is evident then that Laura Foster was murdered in the spring of 1866 during corn planting season. Usually such planting occurred in late April but could be delayed until late May, depending on the amount of spring rain, the industry of the farmer, and the type of seed corn used. It is further evident that Laura Foster was murdered on a Friday. Therefore, it would be safe to state that she was murdered on Friday, May 25, 1866.

(It might be enlightening to point out that free calendars were not available to the people living in the area of the murder until well up into the twentieth century. As late as the 1920's, it was necessary for one to walk two or three miles to the nearest store before he could consult a calendar. Except for the Sabbath, the days were all pretty much alike, filled with labor, and dates were of little importance to the average person. However, this does not explain the discrepancies in the legal documents of the era.)

CAST OF CHARACTERS

TOM DULA

A surprising amount can be learned about Tom Dula, the man, despite the little that is known about him through oral tradition. Information in this sketch comes from his Confederate army record, from the article written by the New York *Herald* reporter, and from statements made by witnesses at the trial, along with some conclusions one might well arrive at by bringing these recorded facts together for the first time.

To begin with, we know that Tom was from poor hill stock and that he might have been literate, an accomplishment for his class and those times. The *Herald* reporter states that Tom himself wrote the note exonerating Ann Melton as well as a fifteen-page "lengthy statement of his life." However, his name on both the prisoner of war record and the Oath of Allegiance (which freed him from captivity) is misspelled and marked with an X, as though the signature had been written by a witness.

Tom's mother testified that he was twenty-two years old on June 20, 1866. His Civil War record indicates that Thomas

C. Dula enlisted at Elkville, in Wilkes County, on March 15, 1862, as a private in Company K, 42nd Regiment North Carolina Infantry, for three years or the duration of the war. This means that Tom joined while still seventeen, three months before his eighteenth birthday. Mrs. Mary Dula also testified that Tom was her "sole remaining boy," since she had lost two other sons in the war. Tom was very likely the youngest of three sons, though it is quite possible for one or both brothers to have been younger than he and to have joined after he did.

Mrs. Mary Dula was a respected woman, very likely a widow, since a father is never mentioned. Rufus Horton, a plantation owner from the Yadkin River aristocrats, testified that Mrs. Dula's general character was good for truth and honesty. There is no indication that she had more than one daughter. She testified once, "I have a grown daughter, Eliza, who lives with me." The *Herald* article relates that Tom Dula's sister and her husband came to Statesville to claim his body and with a message from Tom's mother. It would appear from the evidence that Eliza Dula was unmarried in the spring of 1866 but had married by the date of Tom's execution. Since young women married early in the hills, if they married, it would be logical to assume that she was younger than Tom.

It is pointless to call attention to the various articles which state that Tom Dula belonged to the 26th North Carolina Regiment (infantry, though some call it a cavalry unit), for a while commanded by Colonel Zebulon B. Vance — the reason Vance "went galloping" to Tom's defense. Tom Dula's war record clearly indicates otherwise. It follows, obviously, that he did not play his banjo and fiddle for Colonel Vance around the cheerful campfire nor play in his Johnny Reb band. The record, furthermore, indicates that Tom Dula did not go through the war unscathed, as some modern writers maintain.

His army record shows that Tom Dula's name appears on a Register of Confederate States Hospital, Petersburg, Virginia, containing a list of clothing and accouterments, the record of receipt dated November 1, 1862; the possessions were delivered to the patient on November 24. This obviously indicates that Tom Dula was in the Petersburg hospital from November 1 until November 24, though whether from sickness or wounds is not recorded. However, the 42nd Regiment had seen little action up until this time and was, in fact, on outpost duty, passing the time drilling at City Point and Blackwater, on the turnpike near Petersburg; this would seem to indicate that Tom Dula was sick rather than wounded. (Clark, 793)

Tom is reported as present (with his company) until admitted to Episcopal Church Hospital, Williamsburg, Virginia, on December 3, 1862, "Re Febris" (with intermittent fever) and remained there until he returned to duty on Christmas Day. In December of 1862 the 42nd Regiment was on outpost duty along the Blackwater River from Ivor Station on the Norfolk & Petersburg Railroad to Franklin, engaging in skirmishes with the enemy frequently. Tom Dula's fever might have been a relapse, since he had been released from the hospital in Petersburg only ten days earlier. (Clark 793) A muster roll dated January-February, 1863, lists him as sick in quarters but present, probably from a lingering illness that had already hospitalized him twice for forty-six days. At that time Tom's regiment was in winter quarters at Garysburg, Virginia.

Subsequent rolls indicate that he remained present with Company K until one dated September-October, 1864, reports him as "absent in Hospital at Richmond since August 10, 1864." Again his ailment is not recorded but very likely was the result of wounds. The 42nd Regiment had arrived at Petersburg on June 17, 1864, and had remained there on duty for almost four months, alternating with Colquitt's

Brigade for occasional periods of rest. The 42nd defended the salient on Hare's Hill, the most dangerous point on the entire line. "It was exposed to the constant fire of the mortars, with no chance to retaliate." (Clark 800-801)

Much has been made of the fact that Tom Dula was a musician in the service, the writers always referring to the banjo or fiddle, in using the term. (There is nothing recorded to indicate Tom played a banjo; Pauline Foster testified that he once came by James Melton's house to pick up his fiddle and another time that he played his fiddle until bedtime.) The January-February, 1864, muster roll of Company K does give Tom's rank as "musician," but indicates that he was a "drummer." Generally, the company drummer beat out such commands as *charge* or *retreat* in battle. Dr. Manarin states in a letter that the Confederate soldiers did a great deal of drilling when not in battle and that the duty of the drummer was also to beat cadence for marching during drill.

Immediately after organization of the 42nd Regiment, "great stress was placed on thorough drilling in company, regimental, and brigade tactics." As it moved from camp to camp, the 42nd continued systematic drills under Lt. Colonel John E. Brown, an efficient drill master. By continually drilling his men, they were made "predie" (ready and thoroughly prepared for action). (Clark 792) While in winter quarters on the Darbytown road north of the James River, in 1864, the 42nd received its greatest compliment resulting from its dedication to proficient drilling. General Robert E. Lee requested of General Longstreet the best drilled regiment in his corps to perform the last military honors at the funeral of General Gracie (killed at Petersburg), who was to be buried in Richmond. The 42nd Regiment received the detail. "The movements and evolutions of the 42nd were pronounced faultless . . . The congratulations and praises of military men in the city were generously bestowed, some saying it was the best drilled regiment ever seen in

Richmond." (Clark 801-802) Being the company drummer in such a regiment would have demanded the best of the most qualified man for the job.

In March of 1865, General Hoke's division met the troops under General J. D. Cox (Federal) from New Bern just below Kinston, on the south-east shore of the Neuse River, near Wise's Fork. On March 8, the 17th and 42nd regiments left their line of battle during the night and at dawn were on the flanks of the Federals, driving them back. Between 1,500 and 1,800 prisoners were taken, along with four batteries of artillery. On March 10, an unsuccessful assault was made against the breastworks of the enemy.

This charge probably resulted in Tom Dula's being taken prisoner. His record shows that he was captured "near Kinston" on March 10, 1865. He arrived at Point Lookout, Maryland, from New Bern, N. C., on March 16, 1865. Tom was released (as prisoner of war) on June 11, upon taking the Oath of Allegiance. Apparently he returned immediately to his mother's home on Reedy Branch, bordering on Happy Valley.

The following description appears on the Oath of Allegiance report which he signed: hair-dark brown; eyes-brown; height-5 ft., 9½ in. The reporter for the New York *Herald* described Tom as five feet, eleven inches tall, with dark eyes and dark curly hair. There is an inch and a half discrepancy here between the recorded heights, a meaningless amount, since the reporter very likely made an estimate from some distance away. It would be safe to assume that the prison record is correct. His two years in the Statesville jail could very well have thinned him down, causing him to appear taller to the reporter. There is no conflict between the two descriptions of his eyes and hair; very likely, the reporter did not get close enough to determine that they were brown.

The *Herald* writer goes on to describe Tom as "though not

handsome, [he] might be called good-looking. There is everything in his expression," he continues, "to indicate the hardened assassin — a fierce glare of the eyes, a great deal of malignity, and a calousness that is revolting." Some of this vivid description might be prejudice or it might be for the consumption of the typical *Herald* reader of that time. On the other hand, Tom Dula might have made that impression on the reporter. The long legal battle and the two years of imprisonment, the few moments in the sun on his way to certain death could hardly have left him appearing contrite and noble.

As for Tom Dula's character, there can be little doubt but that he was depraved as we understand the word. And the fact that he was a gallant soldier for over three years has little relevancy in the matter. He was a lecherous young man, a characteristic that did not come about as a result of the war and the uncertain peace.

Lotty (Carlotta) Foster, Ann Melton's mother, testified that two years before the war she had caught Tom in bed with Ann after Ann's marriage to James Melton. Tom jumped out of bed, she stated, and got under it. She ordered him out. She said that Tom had his clothes off. The war started in 1861; two years before, in 1859, Tom would have been fifteen years old, and if the escapade had occurred before June 20 of that year, he would have been only fourteen. Allowing some slight margin of error in Lotty Foster's testimony, Tom still started his lechery at an early age.

Tom Dula's relationship with Ann had started as early as three years before he joined the army and probably began again as soon as he returned to Reedy Branch, in the early summer of 1865. He lived in a convenient location for such a liaison. According to Colonel Isbell's map, it was only a half mile from Tom's mother's home to Lotty Foster's cabin, on a ridge up the branch and beyond the Stony Fork road. James and Ann Melton lived only a short distance beyond Lotty. If necessary, Tom and Ann could have used the woods, which surrounded the narrow valley, but according to the testimony of Pauline Foster, they rarely yielded to such inconvenience, using instead one of the three beds in James Melton's house while he slept.

The testimony of Wilson Foster, Laura's father, indicates that Tom began to cohabit with Laura early in 1866. The father saw them in bed together "once or twice." How Tom came to know Laura is not recorded. She lived five miles away, in Caldwell County, but in a rural area with a scattered population, that was no distance at all to prevent "neighbors" from forming relationships. The easy guess would be that Tom had found out about Laura through her "reputation," the sort of reputation that would have attracted him. And there can be little doubt from the evidence but that Laura Foster was a woman of easy virtue.

How many women of the Happy Valley area Tom Dula had intercourse with other than Ann Melton, Laura Foster, and Pauline Foster can only be surmised (although once he and Ann quarrelled over a Caroline Barnes). There is some proof on record that he carried his lechery into the army with him. The *Herald* reporter wrote that many of his former companions in the army from the mountain region attended the hanging, and among some of them it was generally believed that he (Tom) had murdered the husband of a woman at Wilmington (N.C.) during the war, a woman with whom he had "criminal intercourse." Although he had a strong attachment to Ann Melton, it is clear that Tom Dula was a no one-woman man.

The *Herald* reporter states that it was the opinion of all Tom's former companions who had come to see him executed that he was "a terrible, desperate character, and from their knowledge of his former career an anxiety and singular curiosity was excited among them to see how he died." Tom Dula might have been terrible and desperate, certainly desperate at this stage of his life, but there seems to have been a tender side to him barely glimpsed below the surface of his violence and lechery. The *Herald* reporter wrote that "since the war closed, (he) has become reckless, demoralized and a desperado, of whom the people in his vicinity had a terror." One of the tenderest passages to be found in the trial is when Tom's mother is testifying about bending over Tom while he slept. Certainly, mothers are often blind to the faults of their children, but there appears to have been more than average affection in Mary Dula for her only living son.

The most touching scene in the entire sordid story is sensed through Pauline Foster's testimony, when she recounts how Tom and Ann embraced and wept before Tom fled for Tennessee and how he promised he would return at Christmas for his mother and her. This reaction, coupled with his final gesture, his note exonerating Ann from all guilt in Laura Foster's murder, would appear to reveal an affection for Ann Melton more devoted than lechery, and a softer side to Tom Dula's nature.

Whether or not one wishes to call this affection *love* and to state outright that "Tom Dula loved Ann Melton" depends on the individual's understanding of a word so abstract as to convey very little meaning. Tom Dula regretted leaving Ann Melton so much that he held her in his arms and wept (or did he weep in fear and desperation at his plight? Such a soldier as he apparently had been would hardly react in this manner). When the long fight was obviously lost and he was half way through his last night on earth, Tom did not choose to contribute further to Ann's punishment but exonerated her with a brief note. Would he have behaved in this manner if his feelings for her were or had been lust alone, a lust no longer of any use to him? He very likely would not.

How brave was Tom Dula and how determined was he? Did he give in to his fate, sitting back and allowing his appointed counsel to do all his fighting for him?

Oral tradition maintains that he was a brave man, an excellent soldier whom Zeb Vance was proud of. But we can forget oral tradition in this matter, also, because it has proved so undependable in other aspects of Tom Dula's story. The *Herald* reporter wrote that "he fought gallantly in the Confederate service, where he established a reputation for bravery." Obviously, the reporter had his information from officials and army companions who had known Tom and had served with him. Washington Anderson testified: "I knew the general character of the prisoner while in the army. I was in the same company and regiment. His character was good as a soldier." Even while criticizing his character, none of those who came to his execution suggested that he was anything but brave. In fact, it is implied that that was the very reason for their coming – they were there to see how a man as brave as Tom Dula had been would die on the gallows. And he died gamely. The *Herald* reporter wrote: ". . . The fall was about two feet, and the neck was not broken. He breathed about five minutes, and did not struggle." With the life slowly throttled out of him, it would have taken great willpower, it seems, for Tom Dula to remain so still while dying.

A man who would join the infantry at the age of seventeen and could survive three years of one of the bloodiest and most destructive wars in American History, despite sickness and injury, and end up with his original company when the war was lost was certainly a man more courageous and alert than the average individual. And such a man is not likely to sit back and allow himself to be prosecuted and hanged without exerting any effort to save himself. The fact that he fled into Tennessee is an obvious indication of his willingness to resist. When Tom was captured, he perhaps felt it was futile to oppose Col. Grayson, who carried a gun and was supported by one or two officers, also armed. And he was probably bound the night following his capture, when Col. Grayson's young son guarded him. But we have the *Herald* reporter's statement that Tom tried to escape the next day on the way back to Wilkesboro.

And through the long months he was awaiting trial and awaiting the decisions of the Supreme Court he was not idle. There is no record that he attempted to escape while in Wilkesboro jail or on his trip from there to Statesville. But there was that about his personality and behavior which put the Prosecution at Statesville on guard. At their instance the following Court order was handed down:

> *It appears to the satisfaction of the Court that the insecurity of the jail of said county (Iredell) requires an additional guard for the safe keeping of the prisoner Thomas Dula in said prison. It is therefore ordered by the Court that a guard of eight men be allowed the sheriff of said county for the safe keeping of the prisoner Thomas Dula.*

Paying for eight additonal guards would seem like an exorbitant cost for a county to take on unless the character and determination of the prisoner required it.

As the noose became an inevitable prospect, Tom Dula apparently became more determined and desperate in his attempts to escape. He was kept shackled as his execution date approached. The *Herald* reporter stated that the jailer, before he left Tom the night before his execution, discovered that his shackles were loose, a link in the chain having been filed through with a piece of window glass, which was found concealed in his bed. One acquainted with cutting metal and the effort required to saw a chain link in two, even with a hacksaw, can realize the long hours Tom Dula must have spent working on the metal with a sliver of glass.

Finally, was Tom Dula so "reckless and demoralized," so hardened as to be capable of murdering Laura Foster for the motive attributed to him by the Prosecution? This is a futile question, because the vast amount of circumstantial evidence indicates beyond reasonable doubt that he did, or was equally guilty along with Ann Melton. Aside from that, it is not hard to believe that a young man, somewhat immoral to begin with, had been so corrupted by the years of slaughter with which he had become acquainted during the war that he could murder a woman who had maimed his manhood, about all he possessed in those desperate times. And if the *Herald* reporter came close to revealing Tom Dula's character through interviewing his neighbors and his army companions, it appears evident that Tom Dula was capable of murder, for a motive strong enough to move him to action. The rumor that he had murdered a husband near Wilmington over his unfaithful wife could have been true.

ANN MELTON

Ann Melton was about the same age as Tom Dula and Laura Foster, around twenty-two in the spring of 1866. According to the *Herald* article, she was "the illegitimate daughter of Cariotta (Lotty) Foster," who lived in a cabin near the Stony Fork road and near Reedy Branch. Lotty Foster had one other child, a son, Thomas, who testified in the trial, but she may have had others, because at one point she states that Tom had come to her house after breakfast because "the *boys* had already gone to work." Wade Gilbert, when interviewed, said his grandmother told him "old Lot Foster would frequently get down in the floor dead drunk." Pauline Foster testified that on the Friday Laura Foster was killed, Ann told her that she, her mother, and Tom Dula "had laid out that night and drunk the canteen of liquor." Although her statement was not true, such behavior on the part of Lotty Foster did not seem to surprise Pauline. This was the background Ann Foster Melton was born into and lived in the first fourteen or fifteen years of her life.

The *Herald* reporter said of her: "She is apparently about twenty-five years of age [two years after the murder], is the illegitimate daughter of one Carlotta Foster, and is a most beautiful woman. She is entirely uneducated, and though living in the midst of depravity and ignorance has the manner and bearing of an accomplished lady, and all the natural powers that would grace a born beauty."

Ann Melton was apparently illiterate because she signed the affidavit at Wilkesboro requesting a change of venue with "her mark." But how much of the complimentary passage is exaggerated for the consumption of *Herald* readers is hard to say. True, she lived "in the midst of depravity," but she fitted very well into that environment. Her mother's testimony that she was already married two years before the war, at the age of fourteen or fifteen, and already having illicit relations with Dula indicates something of her moral character. Wade Gilbert stated that his grandmother told him Ann would sell herself for cloth, tobacco, or whatever goods were available to haulers who camped with teams and wagons near her home. This could very well have been true because Wade Gilbert's grandmother married James Melton after Ann's death and was privy to much information not available to others. However, there is in the records no indication that Ann had illicit relations with anyone other than Tom Dula, except for the testimony of Colonel James Isbell, who stated that "it was generally reported Ann Melton indulged in illicit intercourse with others besides the prisoner."

Pauline Foster's testimony at Statesville seems to indicate that Ann cohabited with Tom Dula to the exclusion of even her husband, but whether this practice was the decision of Ann or James Melton is never clear. (In the unidentified testimony of Pauline Foster, she states that Ann told her James Melton had the disease [syphilis], too, and she intended "to have to do with him" and pretend to him that she caught the disease from him.) James Melton owned a one-room cabin with three beds in it. He slept in one, always alone except for the occasions when Tom Dula went to bed with him, waiting until he went to sleep before he joined Ann in another bed or Ann and Pauline Foster together. The point to be made is that Ann seemed to be married more to Tom Dula than to James Melton, and the latter did not seem to care.

Ann Melton was temperamental, demanding, and aggressive. She was apparently also lazy, with no interest in household duties. Although Pauline, as a hireling, was expected to milk the cows and work in the fields with James Melton, Ann wanted her to do the household chores also. The morning Laura Foster disappeared, Pauline prepared breakfast while Ann lay in bed, went to the field, returned to prepare the noon meal, and returned to the field, leaving Ann in bed all the while. This behavior was exceptional enough to carry weight in the trial but apparently not surprising to Pauline, implying Ann's indolence. And the morning Ann attacked Pauline at Mrs. James Scott's house, Ann had become angry because she had wanted Pauline "to milk the cows and get breakfast both," and Pauline had objected.

Later that day, Ann had come after Pauline, at Mrs. Scott's, carrying a club and said to her, "You have got to go home." She pushed Pauline out the door, got her down, and choked her. Her anger stemmed primarily from the fact that Pauline Foster, in jest, she maintained, had told Jack (John) Adkins and Ben Ferguson that she and Tom Dula had killed Laura Foster. Ann told Pauline during their fight that she had wanted to kill her ever since she had made the remark. After the fight, Ann went back twice to "enjoin" Mrs. Scott not to tell what she had seen and heard. Mrs. Scott substantiated Pauline's testimony as to Ann's attack, her choking Pauline and threatening her with a stick.

Mrs. Scott testified further that Ann enjoined her to let it be her dying secret, what had happened there between her and Pauline. Ann also said to her that when she had started out that day to take revenge, she had commenced with her best friend (apparently Pauline). She started to leave Mrs. Scott, then returned and threatened that she would follow her (Mrs. Scott) to hell if she told, and if the story got out, she would know it came from her. In the second trial a witness not identified testified that Ann had told the witness Tom Dula had contracted a venereal disease from Laura Foster, had infected her with it, and she (Ann) intended to have her revenge by killing Laura Foster or having her killed.

In the unidentified testimony, Pauline Foster states that Ann had great influence over Tom Dula. Once she and Tom were going over to beat up a Mr. Griffin. Pauline testified that James Melton was afraid to ask Ann any questions about anything. Ann boasted, Pauline testified, that she could make Dula do anything and that she always kept everybody about her under her (control). On the Saturday or Sunday following Laura's disappearance, Ann said she had killed Laura Foster and commenced "cussing" about the disease, Pauline stated.

Ann threatened Pauline twice, according to her testimony. On the Thursday before Laura's death, Ann told Pauline she intended to kill Laura Foster and if she (the witness) "should leave that place that day or talk about it with anybody she would kill her." Later, when Pauline refused to go with her all the way to Laura's grave, "Ann cussed the witness terribly until they got to the creek [Reedy Branch] and told the witness that 'if she ever told this, she (Ann) would put the witness where Laura Foster was.'" (The two threats appeared in the unidentified testimony of Pauline Foster.)

The foregoing testimony indicates that Ann Melton was a vindictive and temperamental woman, vengeful and capable of violent action. It is within reason to believe that such a person could have incited Tom Dula to murder and could have joined him in the act.

There is a possibility that Ann Melton was more jealous of Laura Foster than angry over the syphilis she had contracted. At least she was capable of jealousy because she had accused Pauline of being intimate with Tom, an accusation which Pauline denied, obviously lying. She only suspected Pauline. She apparently knew about Tom and Laura because Tom had kept the affair no secret; he told Dr. Carter and others where he had contracted syphilis, or where he thought he had. However, in the unidentified testimony Pauline states that she had never heard Tom and Ann discuss Laura although she had heard them quarrel over Caroline Barnes.

Ann Melton was able to go through the two years of confinement in Iredell County jail with little damage to her appearance, if we can believe the *Herald* article. There is no recorded suggestion as to how she was affected by the execution of Tom Dula, although she had wept over Tom's plight while he waited in the Wilkesboro jail, before her own arrest, and had "frequently sent things to him." Her own trial appeared on the docket of fall term of Superior Court, 1868, in Wilkesboro. Apparently it was short and uneventful, the exonerating note written and signed by Tom Dula the night before his execution carrying a great weight. Ann was acquitted. The following article appeared in the Statesville *American* on November 5, 1868:

> *The trial of Ann Melton, charged as an accomplice to the murder of Laura Foster, took place at Wilkesboro, at the later term of the Superior Court, and she was acquitted. The unfortunate woman has suffered about two years imprisonment, and if guilty, she has been severely punished, and the gallows would have added little to her punishment. Thus ends this woeful tragedy.*

Although there is no record of children, Wade Gilbert

stated that Ann Melton had two daughters, Jane and Ida. Ida moved to Caldwell County, and Jane remained in the vicinity of Ferguson, married and had nine sons and daughters, all of them good, decent citizens. He listed their names, but there is little point in recording them here and good reason not to.

For what ultimately happened to the "unfortunate woman," Ann Melton, one must turn to folklore and hearsay. There is no known record available. She lived for a short while after her trial, two or three years. There were tales abroad that she lived long enough to have several babies, both white and black, which she disposed of by throwing into a hogpen. The most persistent story concerning the cause of her early death is that she was injured when a cart overturned and died slowly of injuries over a period of several weeks or months. Just before she died, she was said to have screamed in terror, maintaining she could hear meat frying in hell and see black cats climbing the wall.

Soon after Ann Melton's death, Wade Gilbert's grandmother married James Melton, Ann's widower.

PAULINE FOSTER

Pauline Foster was the "key witness" in Tom Dula's trial, the one on whose testimony the State placed the most emphasis. It would be safe to say the Prosecution's case depended so much on Pauline Foster's testimony that they could not have gained a verdict of guilty without it. In effect, it appears that Tom Dula was hanged as the direct result of Pauline Foster's sworn word. What kind of person was this girl the State depended on so much in meting out justice?

When she began her testimony at Statesville, the clerk identified her "as a young woman." The *Herald* reporter wrote: "Pauline Foster, the principal witness against both the accused, is remarkable for nothing but debasement, and may be dismissed with the statement that she has since married a white man and given birth to a Negro child."

Pauline Foster cannot be treated so lightly; she is too important to be dismissed with one sentence, though that sentence does appear to summarize her character. From her own testimony (at Statesville and from the unidentified fragment) we know that she was a distant cousin of Ann Foster Melton, that her home was in Watauga County, and that she was twenty-one years old. She stated that she came to the Reedy Branch "settlement" the first of March, 1866, to visit her grandfather and that she saw Ann and James Melton, who promised her twenty-one dollars to work through the summer. The money was to be spent for medicines and treatment of "this venereal disease." Apparently, Dr. Carter was her physician. She said she contracted the disease in Watauga County; it is not clear just what her ailment was, but it was probably syphilis. When accused by Ann, in the presence of Mrs. James Scott, of having a disease, Pauline asserted, "Yes, we all have it." *All* undoubtedly included Tom Dula and Ann Melton, (who definitely had syphilis) and apparently James Melton as well; *it* would seem to indicate that Pauline's malady was the same thing. If so, one of the ironies of the entire affair could have been that Tom Dula contracted the disease from Pauline, rather than Laura Foster, and could have in turn infected both her and Ann Melton. In chronological order, Pauline's case appeared first, ahead of Tom's and Ann's, because she came from Watauga County with it the first of March, Dr. Carter began treating Tom for syphilis in "late March or early April," and Ann told Pauline that Dula had given her the pock (syphilis), afterwards.

Pauline Foster appears to have been more promiscuous than either Ann Melton or Laura Foster. At least we have the record of more men involved with her than the other two. Under cross-examination she admits that she had "slept with Tom Dula for a blind," and spent one night in the barn with him. Washington Anderson testified that Pauline spent the night once with him and Tom Dula in the woods. Thomas Foster, Ann's brother, stated that he slept part of "that Friday night" at James Melton's with Pauline. And Ann Melton accused Pauline of having "improper intimacy" with her own brother, an act she denied. Finally, the *Herald* article states that she had married a white man but had given birth to a Negro child, the main import of which is that her husband did not father the child.

There is enough innuendo in these few references to indicate that Pauline Foster was indeed depraved, immoral, and promiscuous. Furthermore, she might have been a drunkard, and certainly did not have much common sense regarding a matter as grave as murder. Ann Melton called her a "drunken fool," when they had their fight. It would have been pointless for Ann to use the epithet *drunken* if there had been no truth at all in the accusation. Of course Pauline could have been drinking when she made her stupid assertion to Jack Adkins and Ben Ferguson, and this could have elicited the remark by Ann. Wilson Foster stated that Pauline had offered to find his mare for him "for a quart of liquor."

Pauline Foster certainly behaved in a foolish manner, involving herself in the murder. A few weeks after Laura Foster disappeared and before the corpse was found, Pauline had gone into Watauga County, but upon her return (Pauline having been persuaded by Ann Melton to come back) told the two men that she and Tom Dula had killed Laura Foster and put her away. She was arrested and questioned before a justice of the peace at Elkville about her statement, but she swore and continued to swear that she had said it "only in jest." However, at the magistrate's hearing she was unwise enough to remark before a witness (possibly George Washington Anderson), "I would swear a lie any time for Tom Dula, wouldn't you, George?"

After Laura Foster's body was found, when Pauline realized she was in deep trouble, she did not hesitate to turn

State's evidence and tell all she knew about the case, and she knew a great deal — enough to assure Tom Dula's execution and to indicate beyond a reasonable doubt that Ann Melton was an accessory both before and after the fact.

(An interesting postscript: the folk pronunciation of Pauline Foster's first name was *Paw*-line and *Pearl*-ene.)

LAURA FOSTER

There is very little on record concerning the description of character of Laura Foster, one corner of the tragic triangle. In the folklore she is the good, innocent young girl who is cruelly murdered, usually by Ann Melton, with Tom Dula looking on or before he can interfere. While growing up in the area, I never heard a word of criticism directed against her and never heard the slightest hint that she was immoral or diseased, the latter condition resulting directly in her death. Wade Gilbert swore vehemently that he had never heard "a word of blame directed against the girl." Folklore also describes Laura as beautiful, with chestnut hair, blue (or green or brown) eyes, and of a friendly disposition.

What did Laura Foster actually look like? The *Herald* reporter wrote that she was "beautiful but frail." She could very well have been frail because the murderer or murderers were able to carry her from a half to three-fourths of a mile at night (according to the prosecution) down a wooded ridge, from the place of murder to the prepared grave. Pauline Foster testified that Laura's teeth were large and that there was a large open space between them; she did not have a missing tooth but "a natural space right in the center of her mouth." None of the other witnesses described Laura Foster, leaving her appearance, so far as recorded information is concerned, uncertain.

It is easier to arrive at some conclusion as to her status and character. She was a poor girl, twenty-two years of age, according to her father's testimony. She lived with her father,

Wilson Foster, at German's Hill, in Caldwell County, and with at least one brother, James. No other brother or sister is ever mentioned, and Wilson Foster testified that her mother was dead. When Laura's body was discovered, it was clothed in two dresses, one "store" clothes and the other "house made." Various witnesses described her shoes as worn, with a hole in them and with pieced heels. Although Wilson Foster did possess a mare, a rare treasure for those times and his class, there is every indication that he was a very poor man and perhaps a tenant on the farm of Wellborne German or Lloyd Jones, who lived near German's Hill.

Dr. George N. Carter testified that he had treated Tom Dula for syphilis and that Tom had told him he caught it from Laura Foster. Wilson Foster stated that Tom sometimes spent the night at his house when visiting Laura and that he saw them in bed together once or twice. The old man was accused by Pauline Foster of saying that he did not care what became of Laura just so he found his mare and that he would kill her (Laura) if he found her. There was no great concern for Laura by her father immediately following her disappearance. That he was more concerned for his mare is implicit in the testimony. Pauline stated that she had suggested to Wilson Foster that Laura might run off with a colored man and he had agreed it might be so. This would seem to imply that Laura was known to have been intimate with Negroes (or a Negro) at a time immediately following their release from slavery, when their social status was extremely low.

Laura Foster's own father apparently did not criticize her for being in bed with Tom Dula in his house, and he apparently would not have been surprised if she had run off with almost any man who came along. There is little reason to believe that she did not infect Tom Dula with syphilis. He was sufficiently convinced of the fact to murder her, if circumstantial evidence can be accepted. If Laura did give him the disease, then she had to contract it from some other man. The foregoing evidence indicates that Laura Foster was a woman of loose morals — at least circumstantial evidence as convincing as that which hanged Tom Dula. And the fact that she was cruelly murdered has no bearing upon this fact.

JAMES MELTON

What kind of man was James Melton, to live with such a woman as Ann and "put up" with her behavior? He was either dense or indifferent, having yielded to Ann's will early in their marriage and moved into his own bed, where he remained. Too, there is some evidence he was weak-willed where Ann was concerned. Pauline Foster testified once that he was afraid to ask Ann anything, and he apparently made no effort to persuade her to work either in the fields or in the house.

One has the impression that he was somewhat older than Ann, although he married her when she was no more than fourteen or fifteen. He was a poor but industrious man, serving the community as cobbler and farming the land adjacent to his one-room cabin. Washington Anderson stated at one point in his testimony that James Melton was a shoemaker, and there are other references in the trial to such work. He made the shoes that Laura Foster was buried in.

As a farmer, he could not afford regular draft animals, either horse, mule, or even ox, and had to yoke his regular milch cows for such jobs as plowing. Pauline Foster stated at one point that after she had milked, "The cows were to be used in the field where I was dropping corn that day, since the ground was not all plowed." Yet James Melton was industrious enough to hire both Jonathan Gilbert and Pauline, the latter living with him and Ann as a field hand and servant; Melton had promised to pay her twenty-one dollars for the summer, a large amount for that time and his means.

There is no record of his testimony, if any, at the trial, although he was paid $16.15 by Wilkes County for appearing as a witness at the trials. All that is known about him is from implication and from statements made by other witnesses. In a community which despised Ann Melton and told dark tales of her evil and lechery for decades after her death, James Melton's name remained unblemished, so much so that a woman of good reputation married him soon after Ann Melton's death.

JAMES W. M. GRAYSON

An interest in the identity of GRAYSON and his connection with Tom Dula is a natural one, since his name is the only man's other than Tom's mentioned in the ballad. Even before he was finally identified, I could not accept the fiction that a local school teacher named Bob Grayson had loved Laura Foster and had done most of the detective work in finding the evidence which convicted Tom. Neither could he have been the sheriff of Wilkes County, as the Winston-Salem *Journal* story stated, since W. G. Hix was the sheriff. Obviously, a Grayson had had something to do with preventing Tom's escape in Tennessee, but what, and who was he, and why did he become involved in the case? More important, where did one start looking for information that might lead to identification? One did not start with the tellers of tales; he started with the legal records, the few extant.

No one named Grayson appeared on the list of witnesses at the grand jury hearing in Wilkesboro nor on later lists directly related to the trials. In fact, Grayson never did appear at either trial because his name is not among those paid by Wilkes County, on the itemized bill of cost the State presented. But what about the two times the second trial was continued? The second trial was first called for the spring session, Superior Court, of 1867, but was continued at the instance of the prisoner because three of his witnesses did not show. The trial appeared again on the docket of fall term, 1867, but this time the State requested that it be continued because three of its witnesses failed to appear. One of them was a James W. M. Grayson (spelled Grason by the Clerk), who was then sitting in legislature in the state of Tennessee.

A letter to the Tennessee State Library and Archives brought a form on James W. M. Grayson, limited in the amount of information available. James W. M. Grayson, according to the form, contested the seat of H. P. Murphy and won in the district of Trade, a small hamlet in Johnson County, near the North Carolina line. He sat in the 35th session of legislature, taking his seat in 1867 and holding it until March 16, 1868. The report gave Grayson's birth date as between 1825 and 1830 and his death at about 1900. He was married to Julia Williams on April 1, 1852.

The form further indicated that James Grayson had been a farmer following the Civil War, "engaged in various enterprises at Grayson, N. C. (a small place just over the Johnson County line)." Scott and Angel's *History of the 13th Regiment Tennessee Volunteer Cavalry* (1903) — supplied in the form — carried the following entry on page 272:

> *James W. M. Grayson was a prominent citizen of Johnson County when the war came and a man at that time of probably 35 years of age. He took an active part as an officer of the Carter County Rebellion, and displayed courage and ability . . . assisted largely in recruiting the Fourth Tennessee Infantry [Federal] and was commissioned Lt. Col. of that regiment May 1, 1863 and through some disagreement with superior officers left that regiment and accepted a commission in the Thirteenth Tennessee as Major, October 6, 1863,*

and remained with the Regiment until 1864, when he resigned on account of ill health.

After the war and up to his death which occurred only a few years ago, he was actively engaged in farming and business enterprises at Grayson, N. C. We know nothing of his family except a daughter, Mrs. Dr. W. R. Butler, of Butler, Tenn., and a son, A. G. Grayson, Esq., who is engaged in business and resides at Trade, Johnson County, Tennessee.

This limited information was a start, but none of it helped to relate James Grayson to Tom Dula, fugitive. Witnesses testified that Tom fled to Watauga County, bordering Wilkes on the west, where he changed his name to Hall, and from there into Tennessee, obviously into Johnson County (which borders on Watauga), where James Grayson was living in the summer of 1866, the time of Tom's flight. The county seat of Johnson County is Mountain City, which has a weekly newspaper called *The Tomahawk*. A letter to the editor stating my problem brought a response from Deane Vennings suggesting that I get in touch with Luke Grayson of Mountain City. J. L. Grayson in the telephone directory turned out to be J. Luke Grayson, 81-year-old grandson of James W. M. Grayson, a man proud of his heritage and eager to help.

J. Luke Grayson was born November 27, 1887, and became a prominent attorney in the vicinity of Mountain City. He was elected District Attorney General of the first Judicial Circuit of Tennessee, which includes Johnson, Carter, and Washington counties, and served for a term of eight years, between September 1, 1934, and September 1, 1942. Retired now, Luke Grayson is still alert and keen of mind. An acquaintance said he was still the best attorney in his area if he cared to practice. It is in his memories of his grandfather and his records that the story of James Grayson's connection with Tom Dula has been preserved.

Following is a summary of Luke Grayson's report on James W. M. Grayson and Tom Dula's capture:

James W. M. Grayson was born in 1833 in Watauga County, N. C., near Sugar Grove. He died in 1900 and was buried in Zionville, in the same area. (Mr. Grayson did not elaborate on James Grayson's military career since I did not request it.) In the summer of 1866, Col. James Grayson was farming at Trade, about ten miles south-east of Mountain City near the state line. Mr. Grayson does not remember the exact date other than that it was June or July, during "farming time"; however, Tom Dula arrived at Trade that summer shoeless or almost so, and remained "a number of days" in Col. Grayson's home, working on the farm as a hired hand in the fields. He was there long enough to earn sufficient money to buy him a pair of boots, which he was wearing at the time of his arrest. J. Luke Grayson's report indicates that the sheriff of Wilkes County pursued Dula into Tennessee, but it is unlikely that the high sheriff would have left Wilkes and the state when he could have sent deputies, especially since Tom had been gone for several weeks when the search for him began. Besides, Jack Adkins testified under oath that he and Ben Ferguson were sent after Dula and brought him back to the county under arrest.

J. Luke Grayson continues, stating that the sheriff came for Dula, but Tom had left a short time before his arrival at Col. Grayson's home. Col. Grayson and the officer (or officers) from Wilkes proceeded to follow him and overtook him at Pandora, in the Doe Valley community, about nine miles west of Mountain City, on the road leading to Johnson City. Col. Grayson dismounted and picked up a rock, telling Dula he was under arrest. It was the gun Col. Grayson carried that probably persuaded Tom Dula to surrender: a seven-shot, rimfire Deemore .32 caliber, which Col. Grayson had worn during the war. (The Honorable J. Luke Grayson still owns the gun.)

After Dula's arrest, Col. Grayson put his prisoner on the horse behind himself and carried him back to Trade, where the fugitive and the sheriff (or deputies) spent the night. "As I understand it," J. Luke Grayson writes, "my father, W. F. Grayson, who was a young boy, guarded Tom Dula for the night." The next morning Col. Grayson and the sheriff (or deputies) took the prisoner back to Wilkesboro, Dula riding behind Col. Grayson, his feet tied beneath the horse's belly.

J. Luke Grayson said that he never had heard that Tom Dula had changed his name to Hall.

Grayson's report concludes with the information that Col. Grayson was among the large real estate owners of Johnson County, Tennessee, and Ashe County, N. C. He was a farmer and trader in real estate and livestock. He belonged to the Masonic Lodge, was a member of the Baptist Church and a successful lawyer who practiced in a number of courts in east Tennessee and western North Carolina.

Col. Grayson did not testify either at the trial of 1866, under Judge Buxton, or the trial of 1868, under Judge Shipp. In fact he was still a member of the Tennessee legislature during the trial of January, 1868, and remained so until March 16. Why he should have been called for the single trial of fall term, 1867, is not clear. However, the summons served one good purpose – it provided the clue which led to his identity.

If it hadn't been for Grayson, Tom Dula might very well have been, or remained, in Tennessee, as the old ballad states.

JAMES M. ISBELL

Col. James M. Isbell, if we may believe the records, was more responsible for finding Laura Foster's body and for the prosecution of Tom Dula than any other individual. Col. Isbell was one of the aristocrats of Happy Valley. He was the great-grandson of Benjamin Howard, through a daughter, Disecretion Howard, who married the first Thomas Isbell, according to Rev. Isbell's genealogy; on his mother's side he was the grandson of Capt. William Dula, and he married Sarah Horton, Daughter of David E. Horton, one of the wealthier plantation owners. James M. Isbell had been a colonel in the local militia but was elected a second lieutenant in the "Rough and Readys," Company A, 22nd North Carolina Regiment, when that company was organized at Lenoir in April of 1861. (*Happy Valley* 97) He spent a short while in service, attaining the rank of captain, but returned home to serve in the state legislature. For the rest of his life he was called Col. Isbell rather than Captain, his regular army rank.

The Isbell family owned at one time a large tract of land extending from the Yadkin River along the east side of Kings Creek for three miles, to the crest of Slick Rock Mountain, behind the community of present-day Grandin. When Col. Isbell's grandfather died in 1865, all this land was sold by the executor to satisfy a note the elder Isbell had signed. At the time of Laura Foster's murder, Col. Isbell was left with only two hundred acres lying where Grandin is now located, land he inherited through his mother. (Isbell, 139)

The murder occurred May 25. The body was not discovered until late August or early September, according to Dr. Carter's testimony, over three months after the burial. Large numbers had formed search parties through the early part of the summer hunting for Laura's grave, without success. It is logical to assume, human nature being what it is, that enthusiasm for the search waned through the hot weeks of late summer and that fewer and fewer citizens of the valleys and hills continued to bother with it. In the unidentified transcript of Pauline Foster's testimony she states that Ann Melton said to her, in late summer, "I want to show you Laura Foster's grave. They have pretty well quit hunting for it."

But for some reason Col. Isbell never lost interest in the search and had induced his elderly father-in-law, David E. Horton, to accompany him the day the corpse was discovered. When Pauline Foster, under arrest in the Wilkesboro jail, told of her and Ann Melton's visit to a pine log on a ridge near Laura's grave, she was taken back to Reedy Branch to guide a search party to the spot. There is no clue as to how many and who were in the group other than Pauline, Col. Isbell, and David E. Horton. The implication is that they split up into groups, perhaps pairs, at the log and searched the area around it. Obviously, Col. Isbell and David E. Horton (Isbell identifies him only as his father-in-law) were alone at the time the grave was discovered because Col. Isbell says, "I was at the grave at the time of the discovery. My father-in-law was with me." And again he says, "My companion's horse snorted and gave signs of smelling something." The point to be made is that Col. Isbell retained his interest in finding Laura Foster's body throughout the summer when almost everyone else had given up, and he persisted until he and his father-in-law made the discovery around the first of September.

It is interesting to note that Col. Isbell was an aristocrat who lived in Caldwell County. He was a justice of the peace, but his jurisdiction would not have extended into the Elkville township, in Wilkes County. He was tied to Elkville and the river land owners by strong bonds of family kinship and by geography; his home was on Kings Creek, a tributary of the Yadkin River, and the people along that stream were closely associated with those along the Yadkin. Why would a man of his birth and position have such a great interest in a murder committed among the hill folk? Why would he search so doggedly over the months until the corpse was finally discovered? In his testimony, he states, "I have assisted in employing counsel for the prosecution. I have no feeling of enmity against the accused. I am influenced solely by consideration of public good." Does this last statement truly answer the question? He lived nine miles from Laura Foster and, even if he knew her, very likely had little personal interest in a girl of her lowly birth and reputation. The answer might be that Laura was a citizen of Caldwell County, as Isbell was, and that he felt a deep interest in seeing justice done.

Whatever his motive, Col. James M. Isbell had considerable responsibility for the discovery of Laura Foster's body and for the prosecution and death of Tom Dula.

DR. GEORGE N. CARTER

Dr. George N. Carter was also one of the wealthy land owners in Happy Valley. Dr. Carter moved to the valley from Ashland, Virginia, in the early 1850's and married Juliette Jones, a granddaughter of Captain William Dula. He owned a fairly large tract of land along Kings Creek, on the west side, which bordered the old Isbell plantation for more than a mile. Apparently Dr. Carter was the only physician for miles around. Rev. Isbell implies as much in his book and never mentions another one other than the elder doctor's son. Dr. George N. Carter served the valley for thirty-five years, and his son, George H. Carter, continued as region physician for forty-five years after his father. (Isbell 9-10)

Dr. Carter was the obvious man to summon to examine Laura Foster's corpse when it was finally found, but nowhere in the records is he called the coroner.

RUFUS (DULA) HORTON

Rufus (Dula) Horton was not important in the case but did testify that Mrs. Mary Dula's reputation was good for "truth and honesty," and that Jesse Gilbert's reputation was bad for "stealing and lying."

Rufus Horton owned a rich plantation adjacent to Elkville and Cowels Store. The son of Gen. William Horton, he had inherited and resided at the old Horton homestead, founded by Benjamin Howard, "one of the best farms on the river." (Isbell 39)

WELBORNE GERMAN

Welborne German "entered" about 200 acres including German's Hill in 1840 and built a house on the east side of the hill, giving his name to the hill and township (a rough hill lying on the bend of the Yadkin River and jutting down to the stream). The community in the area was called German's Hill, and it was here Laura Foster lived with her father and at least one brother. In the early days the community had a store and post office called Cilley (named for Col. C. A. Cilley of Lenoir), but the original name persisted and remains today.

THOMAS M. DULA

Thomas M. Dula, about 1830, acquired all the land from Patterson for two miles down the river on both sides, some 1,500 acres. Whether this is the same Thomas M. Dula the County of Wilkes paid $19.70 for appearing as a witness is not absolutely certain, but could well have been because he lived in the vicinity of German's Hill, near Wilson Foster and Laura.

JAMES C. HORTON

James C. Horton owned a plantation on the south side of the Yadkin River in the vicinity of what is now Ferguson. James was the son of Gen. William Horton and the grandson of Nathan Horton, one of the first settlers on New River, near Boone. (Isbell, 38) James C. Horton received $13.10 for appearing as a witness at the Tom Dula trials.

It is not possible to identify the remaining witnesses in available records.

JUDGE RALPH P. BUXTON

Judge Ralph P. Buxton, who presided at the first trial of Tom Dula, was born in 1826 in Washington, N. C. He was graduated with distinction from the University of North Carolina and later served as solicitor of the Fayetteville Judicial District. Judge Buxton allied himself with the Republicans after the Civil War and was a leader of that party in the upper Cape Fear section of the state. He was a member of the convention for the amendment of the state constitution.

Judge Buxton held his Superior Court bench during the first administration of Governor Holden by appointment but was later elected to the same position. It was during his earlier term on the bench that Tom Dula was tried.

"On the bench," J. H. Myrover, his biographer, said of him, "Judge Buxton was a safe rather than a brilliant jurist . . not that he was mentally slow and plodding, but he was constitutionally careful and accurate." (Ashe V, 43)

The following article appeared in the Salisbury *Watchman and Old North State* on November 5, 1868, copied from the Wadesboro *Argus*:

> *This gentleman is presiding at our Superior Court during the present Term. So far, he has discharged his duties in a dignified, impartial and fearless manner. We are not alone in this opinion. We are sustained on all sides, by parties who have been brought in contact with him.*
>
> *We are more free to give this tribute to the Judge because we know nothing of his political opinions — Whatever they may be he keeps them to himself. He is, we take it, one of the rare few*

who deem it their duty, while occupying judicial positions, to let nothing of politics stain the judicial ermine.

From Ashe's *Biographical History of North Carolina, V.*

JUDGE WILLIAM M. SHIPP

Judge William M. Shipp, who presided at Tom Dula's second trial, was born in Lincoln County in 1819, the son of Bartlett Shipp, a noted legislator and public official. William Shipp was graduated from the University of North Carolina in 1840, second in his class, behind his brother. He was admitted to the bar in 1843.

His early career as a lawyer was spent in Rutherfordton, and he represented Rutherford County in the general assembly of 1854. Moving to Hendersonville in 1857, he was elected as a delegate to the convention held in 1861 which adopted the Ordinance of Secession and was a signatory of that document.

When war began, he raised a company in Henderson County and served as its captain, seeing action until elected a state senator from Henderson in 1861. The following year he was elected judge of the Superior Court from the Lincoln district, serving on that bench with distinction until 1868, when the opposing party came into power.

Judge Shipp moved to Charlotte and was elected Attorney General in 1870, although the Democratic candidates running with him (including the gubernatorial candidate) were defeated. At the end of his term, he returned to Charlotte and private practice. In 1881 he was again appointed to the Superior Court bench by Governor Jarvis, where he remained until his death.

From the Charlotte *Observer*, March 9, 1941.

THE PROSECUTOR AND ASSISTANTS

SOLICITOR WALTER PHARR CALDWELL

Solicitor Walter P. Caldwell was born in Charlotte, N. C. After receiving his degree from Davidson College in 1841, he taught school in York County, S. C., then in Mecklenburg County in North Carolina. He began his study of law in Judge Pearson's law school in 1843. After being admitted to the bar, Walter P. Caldwell became solicitor in county court in 1845. In 1852 he became Master in Equity and Clerk of county court. Solicitor Caldwell became engrossing clerk in the state House of Representatives in 1853. Ultimately he rose to the position of District Attorney (solicitor) in the Sixth Judicial District in 1866, was re-elected under the provisional government, and remained in that office until 1874.

Moving to Greensboro in 1874, he formed a law partnership with L. M. Scott. Having suffered a paralytic stroke in 1886, he died November 22, 1888 in Greensboro.

(From an article, "The Caldwell Family," by J. B. Alexander, which appeared in the Charlotte *Daily Observer* on May 8, 1904, and from the *Alumni Catalogue* of Davidson College, "Class of 1841.")

JOHN MARSHALL CLEMENT

John Marshall Clement, the first of Solicitor Caldwell's assistants, was born in what was then Rowan County, now Davie, on November 1, 1825. His first teacher in Mocksville was Peter Nay, who was reputed to have been one of Napoleon's officers, Marshall Nay. When he was around sixteen, John Clement entered the school of Hugh Hill at Bethany in Iredell County. He had attended two other schools by 1844, when he went North and entered Pennsylvania College, Gettysburg. He remained in college there for two years.

Clement returned home in 1846. He studied law at Richmond Hill and was admitted to the bar in 1848.

After spending one term in state legislature, he devoted the rest of his life to the study of law. Although his practice was wide and varied, embracing a large number of capital cases, in his late years he refused to appear for the prosecution where life was at stake.

He died June 4, 1886.

(From Ashe, VIII, 98-101)

NATHANIEL BOYDEN

Nathaniel Boyden, Caldwell's second assistant, was born August 16, 1796, to John and Eunice Boyden in Conway, Mass. He was prepared for college at Deerfield Academy and attended in succession Williams College and Union College in Schenectady, N. Y., where he graduated in July of 1821.

He began his study of law while still in college. Before coming to North Carolina, he studied his apprenticeship law under a New York attorney, Judah Yearby and under his uncle, the Honorable Moses Hayden.

Boyden taught school at King's Cross Roads in Guilford County while learning the North Carolina code and procedure. Later he taught school in Madison, Rockingham County. In December, 1823, he received his license to practice law in the courts of North Carolina and settled near Germantown, Stokes County, where he remained until his death, November 20, 1873.

In 1830 and again in 1840 he represented Surrey County in the House of Commons (lower house), and in 1844 he represented Rowan County in the state Senate. In 1847 he was elected a member of the Thirtieth Congress (U. S.), and at the expiration of his term declined re-election. Twenty-one years later he was elected a member of the Fortieth Congress, and in 1871 he was appointed Associate Justice of the state Supreme Court, holding that post until his death.

Originally, Boyden was a Madisonian Republican, and when the old Republican Party dissolved, he joined the National Republican party. Upon its decline, he became a Whig, and after that party dissolved, he continued to cling to its fundamental doctrines. He became a (Lincoln) Republican in 1868.

Nathaniel Boyden was shocked and disturbed by the commencement of the Civil War, but once the die was cast, he supported the Confederacy with his wealth, his labor, and his family, one of his sons having fought for the South.

Boyden was important in the provisional government in North Carolina between 1866 and 1868. It is maintained that President Lincoln had already written a directive appointing him provisional governor but was assassinated before the appointment could become effective. In the impeachment trial of Governor Holden, he was one of the governor's counsels.

(From an address by Dr. Archibald Henderson of the University of North Carolina faculty to the State Supreme Court at fall term, 1917, and published in *North Carolina Reports*, CLXIV.)

THE DEFENSE

ZEBULON B. VANCE, (Leader of the Defense)

So much has been written and is known about the life of Zebulon B. Vance, who defended Tom Dula, that there is little need for great detail here. His great-grandfather settled in Buncombe County, N. C., in the late 1700's. His grandfather, Lt. Col. David Vance, fought in the Revolutionary War, and his father, Capt. David Vance, was a soldier in the war of 1812, but never saw action. Such was the Vance heritage.

Zeb Vance was born May 12, 1830, in Buncombe County.

He was chiefly self-educated, except for a year at the University of North Carolina. At an early age he was elected to the state legislature (on the American, or Know-nothing ticket, which was the refuge of many Whigs), followed by membership in Congress, elected on the Whig ticket in 1858, at the age of 28, and again in 1860. As a congressman he was opposed to secession, but once war became inevitable, he became one of the South's most conscientious and capable leaders.

Zeb Vance joined the Rough and Ready Guards (Co. F., 14th North Carolina Infantry) in Asheville on May 3, 1861, as a private but was elected captain because of his qualities of leadership. He never saw action in Company F. While on guard and garrison duty at Suffolk, Virginia, on August 16, 1861, he received the news that he had been elected colonel of the 26th North Carolina (infantry) Regiment, and he immediately joined that unit.

Action was still slow coming. The 26th Regiment was guarding Fort Macon, near Beaufort, when Vance joined it, and from there it went into winter quarters. But early in 1862, Vance and his regiment tasted blood and defeat at the Battle of New Bern. It was a moral victory, however, because Vance's regiment retreated in order and fought so gallantly that the battle enhanced Col. Vance's reputation throughout the state.

The only other action Vance experienced was the Battle of Malvern Hill, in Tidewater, Virginia, on July 1, 1862. This was said by some to be one of the three bloodiest battles of the entire war. Vance led the men of the 26th up to within twenty yards of the blazing muzzles of McClellan's troops before they fell back, decimated. Despite this sanguine victory, McClellan retreated during the night, and the battle was not resumed.

Soon after the war began, Governor John W. Ellis died and Vance was urged to seek the vacant office. Running on what he called the Conservative ticket against the Confederates' choice, an obscure railroad official from Charlotte named William Johnston, Vance won by a landslide and was inaugurated on September 8, 1862.

Zebulon Vance was a good and efficient wartime governor, carrying on a vigorous campaign against the Northern armies while fighting to retain civil rights in the state. He controlled North Carolina's productive complex so efficiently that his state clothed half the Confederate forces in Virginia plus many other units. While other Southern states were in want, the close of the war found North Carolina still in possession of 92,000 uniforms and enough supplies to feed 60,000 troops for five months. (Dowd, p. 490)

Vance was elected for a second term in 1864, running against William Holden, a Raleigh newspaper publisher, and his Peace Party.

During the final days of the war, Vance and his family left Raleigh for Statesville, where they were living when Vance was arrested by federal cavalry on May 13, 1865. He arrived in Washington on May 20 and was imprisoned in the Old Capitol Prison. Vance remained there until July 6, when he was allowed to return to Statesville, restricted in his activities while waiting for a pardon. The following statement is self-explanatory:

Statesville, N. C.
December 26th, 1865

I, Zebulon B. Vance, being in arrest by order of the President of the United States and being admitted to parole within the limits of the State of North Carolina, do hereby pledge my honor faithfully to observe the same and to surrender myself whenever required by his order.

ZEBULON B. VANCE

Vance removed to Charlotte sometime between the 6th and 26th of March, 1866, and on April 2 became a member of a law firm with Clement Dowd and R. D. Johnston. A notice in *The Western Democrat*, a Charlotte paper, dated March 6 stated that Vance was "at home in Statesville." The following advertisement appeared in *The Western Democrat* on March 27:

Z. B. Vance
Attorney at Law
Charlotte, N. C.

Will practice in the Sixth Circuit, and in the Federal and Supreme Courts at Raleigh
March 26, 1866.

The Western Democrat ran this advertisement on April 3:

Z. B. Vance   C. Dowd   R. D. Johnston
VANCE   DOWD   JOHNSTON

Attorneys at Law
Charlotte, N. C.

Having associated themselves together, will practice in the Courts of Mecklenburg, Iredell, Catawba, Davidson, Rowan, Cabarrus, and Union, and in the Federal and Supreme Courts.
Claims collected anywhere in the State.
April 1, 1866.

Specifically, sometime in March of 1866, Zebulon B. Vance began to practice law in Charlotte, about the time Tom Dula contracted syphilis, ostensibly from Laura Foster. Zeb Vance had no connection with this obscure and indigent young hill man other than a common participation in a lost war. Vance himself had been penniless while in Statesville, following his return from prison, and after only a few months of practice could not have built up much of a financial reserve when Tom Dula's case appeared on the docket of Superior Court at Wilkesboro during the fall term of 1866. Tom Dula had no money to hire attorneys. Yet Governor Vance and two capable assistants came to his defense without remuneration and devoted not only hours, but days and weeks to defending the prisoner. So well did they build their case and so expertly pursue it that it came twice before the state Supreme Court before a sentence of death by hanging was finally carried out. Only devotion to a cause could have resulted in the degree of success Vance and his colleagues attained. The most puzzling question associated with the entire affair is — why? The fact that they were "appointed" is no explanation.

Why did Zebulon B. Vance, Civil War hero, ex-governor, private attorney in great need of money, devote so much time and labor to the case of this obscure man from the hills? It was certainly not because he knew Dula, nor because Tom Dula had served in the 26th Regiment and its Johnny Reb band, as tradition maintains, because Tom did not serve in that unit. Was it because Tom had served "gallantly" in the Confederate army? Although Vance used Tom Dula's war record to every advantage he could, that does not seem to be a satisfactory explanation.

George Stevenson, formerly a library assistant in the North Carolina Collection at Chapel Hill, suggested that Vance's motive for accepting the case may have been political. Although Tom Dula was obscure to begin with, the murder trial, for some reason, soon captured the imagination of the regional public and ultimately became of national interest, but Vance was already involved by then. Political parties were in a state of flux during the early days of provisional government in the state, and it would be unwise to say that Vance accepted the case because he belonged to the Conservative-Democrats and was opposing the prosecution because they represented the Republicans. But it is safe to point out that political enmity and alignments did exist, often devoid of political nametags, and that Vance was the opponent of those persons then in power cooperating with the occupying armies. Since the political alignments of the Prosecutor and his assistants have been discussed in their respective sketches and that of Vance's assistants follow, the subject requires no elaboration here; however, the facts indicate that there was a division in political viewpoint between the Prosecution and the Defense in the trial. But another book would be required to fully discuss the political aspects of the case, and even then it is doubtful that a conclusion could be reached.

The point to be made is that for some reason we may never know, Zebulon B. Vance chose to defend Tom Dula (and, incidentally, Ann Melton).

It is easier, however, to bring politics into the trial on a lesser scale than that discussed above. For example, Vance's motion for a change of venue, as stated in the affidavit, from Wilkes to Iredell County was that "the case has been much conversed in said county, has produced much excitement, and the public mind has been prejudiced against them (the prisoners) to such an extant that an impartial and unbiased Jury could not be obtained in said county."

There may have been a more subtle reason for the removal of the trial from Wilkes to Iredell. Although Vance received 1,544 votes in Wilkes in his campaign for governor in 1862 to only 76 for Johnston, his opponent, by 1864 Wilkes County had become the "hard core" of the peace movement. Vance chose Wilkesboro for his first campaign speech, but his reception was not enthusiastic, and he lost that county to Holden by 534 votes to 567. Holden was the peace candidate who hinted that he would attempt to take the state out of the war, while Vance promised only a more vigorous campaign against the enemy. In Iredell County, on the other hand, Vance won by 1,106 votes to only 97 for Holden. It is obvious that Vance had reason to expect an Iredell jury to be, not only more lenient toward any client of his than a jury made up of Wilkes County citizens, but also a jury more compassionate toward a veteran of the Confederate army, one of Vance's strongest defenses.

The historical fact remains that Governor Zebulon B. Vance chose to defend Tom Dula without pay and did so ably and conscientiously; why he chose to do so will probably never be known for certain. A postscript to the case is that he defended Ann Melton, accessory, at the fall term of the Superior Court, 1868, in Wilkesboro, and she was acquitted.

Zebulon B. Vance lived for many years after the Dula trial, becoming governor again and a United States senator, but that is not a part of the Tom Dula story.

From *Zeb Vance* by Glenn Tucker and from various other sources.

ASSISTANTS FOR THE DEFENSE

CAPTAIN RICHARD M. ALLISON

Richard M. Allison, who assisted Governor Vance in the defense of Tom Dula in both trials, was born about 1824, the son of Thomas Allison, one of the wealthier and more influential citizens of Iredell County and western North Carolina. He entered Davidson College in 1836 and was graduated in 1840.

During his early manhood, Allison was the county attorney of Iredell and during the Civil War was captain of a company of cavalry. After the war he continued his practice of law. The grounds for the Seventh Article of Impeachment against Governor Holden was the direct result of legal action initiated by Richard M. Allison.

Allison died April 30, 1884, in Statesville.

From an obituary published in the Raleigh *News and Observer* on May 3, 1884, and from the Davidson College *Alumni Catalogue*, "Class of 1840."

ROBERT FRANKLIN ARMFIELD

Robert Franklin Armfield, who assisted the Defense in the first trial of Tom Dula, was born near Greensboro on July 9, 1829. He attended the common school and was graduated from Trinity College (later Duke University). Afterwards, he studied law and was admitted to the bar in 1845, beginning his practice in Yadkinville.

Armfield enlisted in the Confederate Army in 1861, served as a lieutenant colonel in the 28th Regiment of North Carolina Troops. After the war he moved to Statesville and continued to practice law. He was state Solicitor for the Sixth District in 1862 while on furlough from the army. He was a member of the state Senate in 1874 and '75, serving as president of the Senate in 1874.

Robert F. Armfield was elected, as a Democrat, to the forty-sixth and forty-seventh congresses (March 4, 1879 – March 3, 1883). Afterwards, he resumed the practice of law and was appointed and subsequently elected judge of the Superior Court, serving from 1889 until his retirement, January 1, 1895.

He died in Statesville on November 9, 1898.

(From *Congressional Directory*.)

DAVID MOFFAT FURCHES

David M. Furches, defense assistant in the second trial,

was born in Davie County on April 21, 1832. His father was a county justice of the peace and a farmer. All of David M. Furches preliminary education was acquired at the Union Academy in Davie County. Following attendance there, he studied law under Chief Justice Pearson and was licensed in 1856.

Furches' earliest practice was in Mocksville, the county seat, where he served as county attorney. He moved to Statesville in 1866 and remained there for the rest of his life. He was a member of Andrew Johnson's Constitutional Convention of 1865 and provisional district attorney the same year. A Whig before the Civil War, he became a Republican afterwards, but gained no office as a member of that party.

Furches ran with Judge Buxton and Maj. W. A. Guthrie for North Carolina Supreme Court in 1888 but lost. He was finally elected to that office in 1894.

David M. Furches served as Chief Justice of the state Supreme Court from January 5, 1901 until January 1, 1903. During this time an impeachment attempt was made against him and Justice Douglass, but it failed to unseat them.

In late life, Judge Furches was a member of the law firm of Furches, Coble, and Nicholson in Statesville.

From Ashe, I, 287-291.

MEMBERS OF THE STATE SUPREME COURT

Membership in the state Supreme Court did not vary from the June Term, 1866 through the June Term, 1868, the same justices having studied and passed opinions on both of Tom Dula's trials.

Chief Justice: Richmond Mumford Pearson (1805-1878)

Associate Justices:
   William Horn Battle (1802-1879)
   Edwin Godwin Reade (1812-1894)

   Sion Hart Rogers (1825-1874) was state Attorney General during this time.

   Anderson Mitchell, who presided at the Spring Term of Superior Court, February, 1868, in Statesville, set the new date of May 1 for Tom Dula's execution, after the state Supreme Court failed to find cause for a new trial a second time.

THE LEGAL SIDE OF THE AFFAIR

In reading the following account of Tom Dula's two trials, taken verbatim from the source preserved in the (N. C.) State Department of Archives and History, one must keep a few facts in mind:

1. First, the reader must realize that this is not the complete word-for-word version of what went on and everything that was said during the trial. It is the opinion of Mr. Newton, the current Clerk of the State Supreme Court, that "Verbatim transcripts probably were not made in lower courts as early as a hundred years ago — simply on account of the lack of court stenographers."

Mr. H. G. Jones, Director of the Department of Archives and History, states in a letter dated, 28 July, 1969:

The minute dockets are usually the most complete records of trials, and these were the barest outline in most cases. When an appeal was made to a

*higher court, the attorneys and/or the clerks
involved probably got together and composed a
summary transcript for submission to that court.
Disagreements probably had to be resolved by the
judge or judges involved.*

The first trial summary is in much greater detail than the
second, which is little more than a precis.

In short, you are reading a summary of the trial of Tom
Dula and the barest outline of the testimony of a few of the
key witnesses, the few whose testimony was considered the
most significant.

2. The entire record was written in longhand, some words
   carelessly, and many times I had to resort to studying
   individual letters with a magnifying glass and
   comparing them with those in words I already knew,
   when the meaning was not clear from the context.
   Some proper nouns and legal terms were especially
   hard to distinguish.

3. I have typed the manuscript exactly as it appears in the
   original, except for adding an occasional punctuation
   mark so that a sentence may be more easily understood. Mr. Summers, the Clerk, was careless with his
   punctuation, and the few commas he used makes little
   grammatical sense.

4. Near the beginning of this chapter, I have written (in
   boldface) several lengthy paragraphs linking together
   legal documents which appear in the original microfilm
   without comment. Short phrases (also in boldface)
   have been scattered throughout this section for the
   same purpose.

5. The family name *Adkins* is sometimes spelled *Atkins*.
   John Adkins is often called Jack, and *Tempy* Pilkerton
   is also spelled *Tempe*.

Monday, October 1, 1866, the Fall Term of Superior Court of Wilkes County opened, Judge Ralph P. Buxton presiding. A grand jury of 18, "good and lawabiding men of the county were duly summoned, drawn, and sworn and charged to inquire for the State and of concerning all causes and offenses committed within the body of the said County." They were as follows:

1.	A. S. Rousseau	10.	John H. Ellis
2.	A. L. Hackett	11.	Edward Parks
3.	B. F. Gambill	12.	Joseph Speaks
4.	Harrison Hayes	13.	W. F. Alexander
5.	W. W. Summers	14.	Jas. S. Queen
6.	Wm. Johnson	15.	J. F. Parker
7.	Alfred McNeil	16.	Aron Wyatt
8.	Francis Eller	17.	G. F. McNeil
9.	D. A. Leach	18.	John Wilborn

The most important of these "offenses" was the murder of Laura Foster. The grand jury, with Rousseau as foreman, found a "true bill" against Thomas C. Dula and Ann Melton. The Bill of Indictment read as follows:

North Carolina
Wilkes County

Superior Court of Law
Fall Term 1866

The Jurors for the State upon their oath presented that Thomas Dula, late of the County of Wilkes, not having the fear of God before his eyes, but being moved and seduced by the instigation of the Devil, on the 18th day of June AD 1866 with force and arms in the County aforesaid in and upon one Laura Foster in the peace of God and the State then and there being feloniously, willfully, and of malice aforethought did make an assault; and that the said Thomas Dula with a certain knife of the value of five cents which he the said Thomas Dula in his right hand then and there had and held her the said Laura Foster in and upon the breast of her the said Laura Foster then and there feloniously, willfully and of his malice aforethought did strike thrust and stab, giving to the said Laura Foster, then and there with the knife aforesaid in and upon the breast of her the said Laura Foster one mortal wound of the breadth of one inch and depth of six inches of which the said mortal wound the said Laura Foster, then and there instantly died and so the Jurors aforesaid upon their oath aforesaid, do say that the said Thomas Dula, the said Laura Foster in manner and form aforesaid feloniously, willfully, and of his malice aforethought did kill and murder against the peace and dignity of the State.

And the Jurors aforesaid upon their oath aforesaid do further present that Ann Melton, late of the County of Wilkes, not having the fear of God before her eyes, but being moved and seduced by the instigations of the Devil, before the felony and murder aforesaid by the said Thomas Dula done and committed with force and arms at and in the County aforesaid to wit, on the day and year aforesaid did maliciously, feloniously, violently, and in her malice aforethought stir up, move, abet, and cause and procured the said Thomas Dula to do and commit the said felony and murder in manner and form aforesaid against the peace and dignity of the State. And the Jurors aforesaid upon their oath aforesaid do further present that Ann Melton late of the County aforesaid well knowing the said Thomas Dula to have done and committed the said felony and murder in manner and form aforesaid, afterwards to wit: on the day and year aforesaid with force and arms, at and in the County aforesaid, him the said Thomas Dula did then and there feloniously, willfully, and of her malice aforethought receive, harbor, maintain, relieve, comfort, and assist against the peace and dignity of the State.

The following witnesses from the vicinity of Elkville, area of the murder, testified before the grand jury:

1. Dr. George N. Carter
2. James Melton
3. Wilson Foster
4. Carl Carlton
5. Hezekiah Kindall
6. Lotty Foster
7. Thomas Foster
8. Martha Gilbert
9. John Atkins
10. Drewry Atkins
11. Bennet Ferguson
12. Pauline Foster
13. Celia Scott
14. Betsy Scott
15. C. C. Jones
16. Docia Witherspoon
17. Carson Dula
18. James Foster
19. Washington Anderson
20. Thomas M. Isbell

All the witnesses were from Wilkes County except Wilson Foster, the father of Laura Foster, and James Foster, her brother. A Writ of Capias was issued to the sheriff of Caldwell County for them to testify in behalf of the State in the case.

By leave of the Court, the solicitor, W. P. Caldwell, entered a Nollie Proseque as to the third count in the Bill of Indictment, which charged Ann Melton as an accessory after the fact, and this charge was dropped.

The preliminaries having been settled, Thomas Dula and Ann Melton were "brought to the bar of the Court in their proper persons by the sheriff of Wilkes County, in whose custody they were" and the Indictment read to them. After the Indictment was read to the prisoners, they pled not guilty and placed themselves "for good and evil" upon the County and Solicitor Caldwell, who for the State, called for a trial before a Jury of good and lawful men by whom the truth of the matter might be known. Tom Dula and Ann Melton were remanded to Jail until their trial began.

The first act of the defense after the trial began, on

Thursday, October 4, was the presentation of an affidavit requesting a change of venue:

In this case Thomas Dula and Ann Melton make oath they do not believe they could have a fair and impartial trial in the County of Wilkes for the reason that the case has been much conversed in said County, has produced much excitement, and that the Public mind has been prejudiced against them, to such an extent that an impartial and unbiased Jury could not be obtained in said County.

Sworn to and subscribed
to before me in open
Court this 4th day of October 1866
     *G. H. Brown C. S. C.
     [Clerk of Superior Court]
     [*George]

            T. C. Dula
             his
       Ann X Melton
          Mark

In response to the affidavit, the Court ordered that the case be moved to Iredell County for trial and that it be set for trial on Friday of Fall Term, 1866, of the Superior Court of Law for that county. The Court further ordered the sheriff of Wilkes County to deliver the bodies of the prisoners, Thomas Dula and Ann Melton, to the sheriff of Iredell County at Statesville on Thursday of the next term of the Superior Court for that county.

The transcript of the proceedings at the Wilkes County term of Superior Court relating to Tom Dula and Ann Melton, including the transfer to Iredell County, was dated October 10, 1866, and signed by G. H. Brown, Clerk of the Superior Court of Wilkes.

A Superior Court of Law and Equity was opened for the County of Iredell at the Courthouse in Statesville on the seventh Monday after the last Monday in August of 1866, that is, on October 15, the Honorable Ralph P. Buxton, Judge, present and presiding. This is the same judge who had presided in the case two weeks before, in Wilkes.

The transcript of the activity which had occurred in the Wilkes Superior Court in every particular, including the Bill of Indictment and other details, was presented to the Court at Statesville. The first order of the Court was that the Sheriff of Iredell County summon a special venue of one hundred freeholders to appear on Friday morning [Oct. 19] at half past ten o'clock to serve in the case. The following jurymen were selected and served during the first trial:

1.	J. A. McFarland	17.	Thomas Davidson
2.	John S. Morrison	18.	A. C. Sharpe
3.	Edwin Falls	19.	S. J. Brown
4.	John A. Haynes	10.	Wm. A. Morris
5.	William Clark	11.	John C. Barkley
6.	George W. Webber	12.	Jacob Parker

The first motion by the Counsel for the Defense was for a severance in the case. This the Court granted as a result of the following affidavit:

> In this case Thomas Dula maketh oath that he cannot have a fair and impartial trial, if tried jointly with his co-defendant, Ann Melton, for the reason that as he is informed and believes there are important confessions of his co-defendant Ann Melton which will be given in evidence in this case if there is a joint trial and which confessing will greatly prejudice the minds of the Jury against this applicant.

Sworn to and subscribed before me   Tho. C. Dula
this 19th day of October 1866.
C. G. Summers Cleark

Ann Melton remained in jail throughout the first trial and the almost two years of maneuvering that followed. She was present in court during the two trials but never testified, although her statements to others regarding the murder were placed in evidence. From this point on Tom Dula faced the jury alone.

In opening the case, the Solicitor stated that he expected to: prove the charges against Tom Dula by circumstantial evidence, that he expected to show that a criminal intimacy had existed between Tom Dula and Laura Foster, the deceased, a young girl; also between the prisoner and Ann Melton, a married woman who was the wife of James Melton. He expected to show further that the prisoner had contracted a venereal disease from the deceased and had communicated it to Mrs. Ann Melton; that he had uttered threats against the deceased because of the disease; that a day or two before the disappearance of the deceased, the prisoner was seen in close conference with her. He expected to show further that the day before her disappearance the prisoner was seen with a mattock in his hand near the spot where her grave was afterwards discovered; that the night before Laura Foster's disappearance both the prisoner and Ann Melton were absent from their houses; that the morning of Laura's disappearance from her father's house being 28th May 1866 [actually, a Monday, not a Friday] she was seen by a witness at a very early hour riding along the road on her father's mare with a bundle of clothes, in the direction of the Bates place and that the same morning the prisoner was seen going in the same direction by a path leading from Laura's home to the Bates place. The Solicitor would show that there would be evidence the deceased reached the Bates place from the circumstance that the mare returned home with a part of the halter on her, and that the missing part was afterwards discovered tied to a tree near the spot indicated; that from indications of blood discovered, this spot was the place where the deceased was killed. He would show that after search was instituted Dula fled the county; that the grave was discovered by disclosures made by Ann Melton, who on a certain occasion undertook to show it to a witness; that it was so carefully concealed as to defy search for a long time, in its immediate vicinity; that it was at last indicated by the snorting of a horse, which smelt the blood. He would show that when the grave was opened, Laura's body was discovered — also the bundle of clothes with which she left home weeks before; that she had been stabbed through the heart and put in this hole [grave], which was more than half a mile from where she was killed and which was within a few hundred yards of the prisoner's house and within a hundred or two yards of the spot where the prisoner was seen with the mattock in his hand the day before the Friday on which Laura disappeared. By these circumstances and others, the Solicitor stated he expected to prove that Thomas Dula, the prisoner, committed the murder instigated thereto by Ann Melton, who was prompted by revenge and jealousy.

Following are the testimonies of the various witnesses for the State. The testimony was interrupted occasionally by objections; most of these will not appear here but will be presented later.

COL. (JAMES M.) ISBELL

Col. Isbell testified that the annexed diagram marked Exhibit A (a crude map he had made of the area) which was used in the trial, was a faithful representation of the various locations designated, that he was well acquainted with the neighborhood and had made the map himself, that the various places and the distances put down were correct, that Wilson Foster, the father of the deceased, lived in Caldwell County, that the prisoner, Dula, and James Melton, husband of Ann, lived in Wilkes County, that Elk Creek was the dividing line between the two counties in this vicinity.

WILSON FOSTER

Wilson Foster testified that he was the father of Laura Foster. She lived with him. Her mother was dead. He was well acquainted with the prisoner, who commenced visiting at his house two months before the disappearance of Laura. He came to see Laura, who was 22 years of age and unmarried. [He] came sometimes once a week and sometimes stayed all night. The witness had seen him sitting by her side and once saw him in bed with her.

Laura left his house one Friday morning the past May. The prisoner had been at the witness's house the Sunday before and had stayed about an hour, talking with Laura. He had returned on Wednesday before that Friday. The witness had been away when the prisoner arrived but upon his return home, had found Dula and Laura sitting tolerably close together by the fire. This was around twelve o'clock, noon. Dula had left before dinner [noon meal].

The night before she disappeared, the witness went to bed, leaving Laura still up. About an hour before daybreak, she got up, went outside and stayed a few minutes. When she came back in, she went to the closet and he thought she opened it. He then thought she went to bed again. When he awoke afterwards, he found Laura was not in her bed. This was about daybreak. He looked out and found his mare gone from the tree where she was usually tied up at night, since there was no stable. The rope with which she was tied was also gone. He looked for the mare's tracks. One of them was peculiar because he had started to trim the hoof but had left

[it] unfinished with a sharp point to it. He found the track and followed it along the road leading from his house by A. Scott's house to the Bates place. He had followed the track until he got to the old field at the Bates place, where he lost it.

He had gone to James Scott's place for breakfast, then went to James Melton's. He got there around eight o'clock. Ann Melton was still in bed, her clothes off. He had remained there about a quarter of an hour, then visited several houses without hearing anything about his daughter's whereabouts. He had spent that night at Francis Melton's house; when he reached home the next morning, he found his mare there. The rope on her had been broken, about two feet left dangling from her halter, the end "frazzled up."

About four weeks later, he had found the other piece of rope tied to a dogwood tree at the Bates place; the ends of the two pieces of rope had fitted. He knew it was the same rope, since he had made it himself. He found the missing rope about 75 yards from where "I had lost the mare's tracks in the old field. The dogwood to which it was tied was in the bushes."

I [later] saw the corpse of Laura — knew it by the teeth and by the shape of the face, which looked natural. I recognized her clothes. She had on two dresses — one store clothes, the other house made. I knew her shoes. [They] had a hole in them which I remembered. James Melton made them. I recognized her fine-tooth comb. Before leaving home she had boils about her shoulder. The prisoner never came to my house after Laura disappeared.

In response to cross-examination, Wilson Foster testified: It had been some two months since the prisoner had visited at my house previous to the Sunday before she disappeared. [My] recollection is not distinct as to the time. When at James Melton's for the second time on that Friday [Laura disappeared], I did not say that I didn't care what became of

Laura just so I found the mare; nor did I say that I would kill Laura if I found her.

MRS. BETSY SCOTT

Mrs. Betsy Scott testified as follows: I saw Laura on the Friday morning she was missing. She was riding her father's mare bareback with a bundle of clothes in her lap and was coming from her father's past A. Scott's house, where I met her in the road.

(Here it was proposed on the part of the State to offer in evidence the conversation which ensued between the witness and Laura, while on her journey, as explanatory thereof. It was objected to by the prisoner. The objection was overruled.)

The evidence was admitted as follows: I asked Laura if Mr. Dula had come. She said yes, he came just before day. I asked where he was. She said he had gone around to flank Manda Barnes'. I said if it was me, I would have been further on the road by this time. She said she had started as soon as she could. I asked where she expected to meet him. She said at the Bates place.

The witness further stated that these questions were asked her in confidence of a communication made to her by Laura a day or two before. I saw Dula on the Wednesday before that Friday some three miles from Wilson Foster's house, she testified. He was on foot.

CARL CARLTON

C. Carlton testified: I saw the prisoner on the Friday morning of Laura's disappearance. He was on the path which leads through my yard towards the Bates place: It was early, a little after sunup. He stopped in my yard and after a few words with me started off, asking as he left if the path led to

Kendall's. He came from the direction of Wilson Foster's and was on foot.

HEZEKIAH KINDALL

Hezekiah Kindall testified as follows: I saw the prisoner on that Friday morning about eight o'clock between Kendall's and Carlton's going in the direction of the Bates place. I asked him if he had been after the woman. He said no, I have quit that. He was walking. His pants seemed wet with dew.

Under cross-examination the witness stated that from Foster's house to Dula's the way he was going, was as near as any.

MRS. JAMES SCOTT

Mrs. James Scott: I saw the prisoner on that Friday morning after breakfast. He was walking. I asked him to come in. He declined, saying he wanted to see my brother, Washington Anderson. He sat on the steps a few minutes and left in the direction of James Melton's.

PAULINE FOSTER

Pauline Foster: I saw the prisoner early that Friday morning at James Melton's house. I had started out to the field to plant corn. Seeing the cows coming, I went back to the house to get the milk vessels. When I got back to the house, Dula was in the house, leaning over Mrs. [Ann] Melton talking to her in a low voice. She was in bed. He asked me what I was going to do that day. I said I was going to drop corn [drop corn in a furrow and cover it to plant it]. He replied that it was too hot to work. I had one cow to milk, and when I came back he was gone.

I saw the prisoner on Thursday morning, the day before. Ann Melton had gone off from the house, and he came from the direction she had gone. He asked me for some alum, said his mouth was sore. He said he had met Mrs. Melton up on the ridge and had asked her for some [alum], and she had told him to get it at the house. He also said he wanted to borrow a canteen. I gave him one. He gave it to Carson McGuire and told him to get it filled with liquor. I afterwards saw it at the house, filled.

Under cross-examination the witness testified: It was after breakfast on the Friday, some eight or nine o'clock, that Dula came. The cows were to be used in the field where I was dropping corn that day, since the ground was not all ploughed. It was before breakfast on the Thursday when he was there for the alum. I understand the Bates place and the Shop place to be the same. It is in the direction of sunrise from James Melton's; I think I could have seen Dula that Friday morning while I was milking if he went towards the Bates place. I had got about a hundred yards from the house when I met the cows. I planted corn that day along with James Melton. He had gone to the field that morning before I did.

LOTTY FOSTER

Lotty Foster testified: I am the mother of Mrs. Ann Melton. I saw the prisoner at my house on Thursday before Laura Foster disappeared. He came from James Melton's. He asked to borrow a mattock. He got it and started off in the direction of his mother's house. I did not see the mattock again under three or four days. I sent for it twice, and got it the second time. I saw Dula again at my house on that Thursday. Ann Melton was there also. Dula came after dinner [noon meal], and Ann was there before he got there. Both left about 3:oo p. m. The next day, Friday morning, Dula came again from the direction of James Melton's. It was after breakfast. The boys had gone to their work. He asked for milk, and I gave him a half gallon. He took it and left towards home. I saw him afterwards that day late in the evening going towards the Bates place. He did not speak on that occasion. I noticed two places of a little digging [where digging had occurred] on the pathway towards Dula's mother's house. This was 200 yards from the grave. I raised Ann Melton —

(It was here proposed by the State to prove acts of criminal intercourse between the prisoner and Ann Melton. The evidence was objected to by the prisoner. The objection was overruled.)

The evidence was admitted as follows: Two years before the War [Civil War] I saw Ann Melton, after she was married, in bed with Dula. I recognized him. He jumped out and got under the bed. I ordered him out. He had his clothes off.

(The prisoner excepted to testimony.)

I have frequently seen him go in the direction of James Melton's, night and day. I did not know where he was going.

Under cross-examination the witness admitted that there were other young women living up in the direction of James Melton's besides Ann.

MARTHA GILBERT

Martha Gilbert testified: On the Wednesday or Thursday before the Friday of Laura Foster's disappearance I saw the prisoner on the road between Mrs. Dula's and Lotty Foster's. He had a mattock and was skelping alongside the path with it. I asked him what he was doing. He said he was fixing the path and making the road wider so he could go along of nights. It was between 200 yards and 300 yards from where I saw him standing to the grave.

When cross-examined, the witness testified as follows: It was about 100 yards from where he was standing to Mrs.

119

Dula's, his mother's [house]. It was above the old field toward Lotty Foster's.

THOMAS FOSTER
(Brother of Ann Melton)

Thomas Foster testified: On the Thursday before the Friday [on which Laura disappeared] the Prisoner came to the house of my mother, Lotty Foster, and wanted to borrow a mattock. He said he wanted to work some devilment out of himself. I saw him with the mattock going toward his home. It was after breakfast that he came after the mattock.

I saw him afterwards that day passing along. On the next day, Friday, after breakfast awhile I saw him coming towards James Melton's. He was on the Stoney Fork Road before the turning-off place to the Bates place. This was on Friday also. I saw him again on the same day, about sundown, going in the same direction. A quarter of an hour after he passed this last time, I got a horse and went to James Melton's. Dula was not there; Ann Melton was.

In response to cross-examination: A person passing our house could go to either James Melton's or the Bates place.

DR. GEORGE N. CARTER

Dr. Carter testified: About the last of March or first of April last, the prisoner applied to me for medical treatment. He had the syphilis. He told me he caught it from Laura Foster. The latter part of August or first of September, upon a ridge within one half or three-fourths of a mile of Lotty Foster's house in Wilkes County, I saw and examined the dead body of a female, at the spot where it was found. There was a place cut through her clothes; taking off the clothes, [I discovered] in a corresponding position on the left breast, a cut through into the body between the third and fourth ribs. If the knife had gone straight in, it would have missed the heart. If the handle [of the knife] had been slightly elevated, the blade would have cut the heart. The body was lying on its right side face up. The hole in which it lay was two and a half feet deep, very narrow, and not long enough for the body. The legs were drawn up. Such a wound, supposing it not to have penetrated the heart, would not necessarily be fatal, though of a dangerous character. If it had penetrated the heart, it would have necessarily been mortal. The body was in so decomposed a condition, [that] I could not ascertain whether it [the knife] had cut the heart or not. The clothing around the breast was in a rather rotten condition. A bundle of clothes was in the grave.

R. D. HALL

R. D. Hall testified that the prisoner, one day about the middle of May last, at my house as he was coming from preaching, said to me that he was diseased and [he] was going to put them through who diseased him. I replied, Tom, I would not do that.

J. W. WINKLER

J. W. Winkler testified: There was a general search made for Laura Foster. I searched seven or eight days myself. One Sunday, four weeks after her disappearance, the neighbors were all out [and] formed a search line like a line of battle. We searched in sight of the Dula house. I never saw him [prisoner] engaged in the search. We searched about the Bates — or Old Shop place. I saw a rope near there tied around a dogwood. I did not find it myself but saw it soon after [it was found]. The branches of the tree near the dogwood appeared to be nipped off. The end of the rope appeared to be chewed. It was of flax and corresponded with the other end [of the rope bridle on Wilson Foster's mare]. I think the rope we found was Foster's. I had seen his mare tied with such a rope before.

Some two hundred yards from the dogwood tree, on the same side, that is the left side, of the Stoney Fork Road, I saw another place where there were signs of a horse having been hitched. Near this place was a discolored spot of ground, over which twigs had been pulled. The bushes near had been broken off and appeared to be hanging down. The discoloration of the ground at this spot extended the width of my hand. The smell of the earth was offensive and differed from that of the surrounding earth.

I knew Laura Foster. I saw the dead body. I thought from her cheekbones and her teeth and from the dress that it was her body. It had on a homespun dress which I thought I knew.

In response to cross-examination: Laura's teeth were large. I don't think there was any space between them. I saw no horse track around the dogwood tree. I think part of the time and most of the time we were searching that Dula was in jail. The so-called blood spot was out of reach of the whiteoak, to which the horse was tied the second time as we thought. It was some fifteen or twenty feet off from the whiteoak. I thought the discolored spot was blood; I supposed so from what I concluded was an attempt at concealment. I think it was a mile or three-fourths [of a mile] from the blood spot to the grave. [I was] never at the grave but knew the ridge where it was found.

PAULINE FOSTER

Pauline Foster: I was staying at James Melton's as a hireling (witness is a young woman). I went there for the first time in March last. Dula was at the house. He was there most every day while [I was] in the settlement. He stayed there sometimes at night. I have seen him in bed with Ann Melton, wife of James Melton, frequently. There were three beds in the room. James Melton did not sleep with his wife. The prisoner would slip to bed with her after she had gone to bed. He would first lay down with James Melton.

Ann Melton became sick. The remedies she used were blue stone, blue mass, and caustic.

(Here it was proposed by the state to show by this witness what Ann Melton had said was the matter with her and who had occasioned her sickness. This was objected to by the prisoner but admitted by the Court. The witness then stated that Ann Melton told her, not in the presence of Dula, however, that Dula had given her the Pock [a provincialism for syphilis]. This was said about a month after the witness went to live at the Melton's and previous to Laura Foster's disappearance.

The prisoner excepted.

The witness continued her testimony: Ann Melton left her husband's house on the Thursday before that Friday in May after dinner [noon meal] with a canteen of liquor, which had been filled for the prisoner, and went in the direction of the Ridge Road. She was absent from that time until an hour before day on Friday. She came and got in bed with me. I left her in bed when I went to work. Her dress was wet and so were her shoes. She lay in bed until after breakfast. This was the morning I mentioned that Dula stood over her and talked with her while she was in bed. When I came to get dinner [noon meal], Ann Melton was on the bed and remained so until I left for the field. I stayed in the field at work with Jonathan Gilbert and James Melton until three o'clock.

Wilson Foster came to James Melton's about dark Friday night and left two or three hours in the night [after nightfall]. Thomas Foster was also there and stayed all night.

I sat up with him until midnight. On Saturday morning, Dula came early. He and Ann Melton conversed together in a low tone for half an hour. He said he came for his fiddle and to get his shoes mended. I remarked to him, "I thought you had run away with Laura Foster." He laughed and said, "I have no use for Laura Foster." He left for home. Dula came there again that night and stayed all night. He went to bed with James Melton. Dula was there every day or night after that as long as he remained in the settlement. He remained in the settlement some four weeks after the disappearance of Laura Foster and then left for Tennessee.

(Here, it was proposed by the State to offer in evidence the conduct of Ann Melton the evening previous to the departure of the prisoner to Tennessee. This was objected to by the prisoner for the reason that according to the theory of the state, the murder of Laura Foster was at that time an accomplished fact; which murder the state charged was perpetrated by the prisoner, incited thereto by Ann Melton. Any conduct of Ann Melton after the accomplishment of the alleged crime could not have contributed to the accomplishment and therefore ought not to be admitted against the prisoner, who was now alone on trial. It was also distinctly stated by the prisoner's counsel that they made this objection in advance to the exception of evidence of any act of Ann Melton, not now on trial, done by her or word spoken by her after the alleged time of the murder, as such acts and words could not have been done and spoken in furtherance of the common alleged design. Objections by prisoner were overruled by the Court.)

The witness continuing, testified that the afternoon before the prisoner left the neighborhood, Ann Melton went to the head of the [her] bed and tore off a clapboard from the log side of the house and scraped the dust off and made a hole through the chinking. She then drove a nail in the log outside, put a string through the hole, tied one end to the nail and put the other end in bed. She also put a knife under the head of the bed.

(Here the prisoner excepted.)

Thomas Dula came a little after dark. He waked James Melton and came in [the house] afterwards. We sat up until bedtime. I offered to fix a bed for Dula, but he declined. He threw himself across one of the beds with his clothes on. Mrs. Ann Melton lay down on my bed. I got in behind her. I found she was crying. After a while, he [Dula] came from his bed, which was at the foot of ours, into ours, getting in on the outside from me. I heard them both sobbing. Ann Melton arose and went outside; he followed her. Afterwards he came back and raised up the head of the bed. I asked him what was the matter. He said, "Come outside and I will tell you." I went out, and he said they were telling lies on him and he had to leave. He said he was coming back for Ann and that he would take her away with him. They embraced and parted in tears. This was four weeks after Laura Foster's disappearance.

Two or three days before their parting, I heard James Melton say in the presence of the prisoner that "it was reported about [by the] Hendricks[es] that Dula had killed Laura Foster." Dula laughed and said, "They would have it to prove and perhaps take a beating besides."

(Here, the State proposed to show by the acts of Ann Melton without calling for her declarations that she undertook to accompany the witness to the grave of Laura Foster and did in fact accompany her to a point within one hundred yards thereof and at that point did cover with leaves a spot of ground where the soil had been disturbed. The prisoner objected to this for the reason alleged in the fourth exception. The objection was overruled and the evidence was admitted by the Court.)

The witness stated that on one occasion after Dula was in jail on this charge, at the instance of Ann Melton, I started with her from the house of James Melton. We went by Lotty

125

Foster's, crossed the Reedy Branch, went through an old field onto a ridge up to a log. Here Ann Melton picked up an apron full of leaves and placed them on a place by the log that appeared to have been rooted about. The place where we stopped was one hundred yards or a little more from the grave as it was afterwards discovered. We were going in that direction [of grave] when I became frightened and refused to proceed.

(The prisoner excepted.)

I saw the dead body. I thought it was the body of Laura Foster. I recognized her teeth and dress. Her teeth were large and there was a large open space between them. I had seen the dress before it was made up. It was woven with a single slay.

In response to cross-examination: I hadn't seen Laura Foster since the first of March. It was nearly three months between that time and the discovery of the body. The heels of the shoes on the corpse were worn and pieced. There was a hole in one of the shoes, in the side of the toe. Laura's tooth was not out, but there was natural space right in the center of the mouth.

Dula came to James Melton's on Thursday before the Friday of Laura's disappearance before breakfast and left without breakfast. This was the time he got the alum and canteen. Ann Melton remarked when she went off on that Thursday with the canteen that she was going to her mother's. She didn't come back until Friday morning early. She was home all day Friday. Dula came there but one time that day. I didn't go off the place that day.

Wilson Foster, Thomas Foster, William Holder, and Washington Anderson were there at James Melton's on that Friday night. We were all joking that night. Thomas Foster burned the old man's [Wilson Foster] whiskers. Thomas Foster did not sleep with me that night. I got in bed with Ann Melton.

I admit I have this venereal disease. I got it in Watauga County and came to James Melton's to get cured and worked with him for money to buy medicines. Ann Melton is a distant relative of mine. I did go to meet a Negro boy near the road, who was sent for me by Mrs. James Scott. The boy gave me a message from Laura Foster. I was arrested and sent to jail for what I said in jest to Jack Atkins and Ben Ferguson. I had been over into Tennessee and after my return, one evening, Ben Ferguson said to me that I had killed Laura Foster. I replied, "Yes, I and Dula killed her and I ran away to Tennessee." I told James Melton I had this conversation with Ferguson and Atkins as a joke, and he told me not to joke about such a thing. I was arrested two or three weeks after I had made this remark.

I did have a fight with Ann Melton on that occasion [an occasion mentioned in the trial]. Ann said to me, "You drunken fool, you have said enough to Ferguson and Atkins to hang you and Tom Dula." I admitted then that I had said it, but had said it in a joke. I admit I said on one occasion to George, "I would swear a lie any time for Tom Dula, wouldn't you, George?" I said this also in jest.

I have been twice sworn as a witness about this matter — once at Wilkesboro and again after the body was found. I deny that I ever told James Melton that it was true I had killed Laura Foster. What I told him, I have stated. It is true that I sat in Dula's lap for a blind, one day when a woman came to James Melton's. Dula caught me and pulled me into his lap. I also slept with Dula for a blind at Ann Melton's insistance. I stayed out at the barn one night with him at his request. There were three beds in James Melton's house. The house had but a single room. Sometimes when I was sleeping with Ann Melton, Dula would get in bed with us also. James Melton did not sleep with his wife. I did hear old man Wilson Foster say that if he could get his mare, he didn't care what had become of his daughter.

I might have told him that I could find his mare for a quart of liquor. If I said so, it was in jest. I did suggest to Wilson Foster that maybe a colored man had run away with Laura, and he said that might be so. I also said that I would sooner have supposed that someone up in her neighborhood would have run away with her than Thomas Dula.

Direct examination resumed: The reason I said I supposed perhaps a colored man had run away with Laura was in consequence of information I received from others, and so as to the other supposition —

(Exception: Here, it was proported on the part of the State to give in the acts and declarations of Ann Melton on the occasion of the fight between her and the witness at Mrs. James Scott's, alluded to in the cross-examination. The prisoner objected for the reasons advanced in the fourth exception. Objection was overruled and evidence was admitted by the Court.)

The witness states: After I had made the remark to Ben Ferguson and Jack Atkins, I and Ann Melton had a quarrel. I went over to the house of Mrs. James Scott. Ann Melton came there with a club and said to me, "You have got to go home." She pushed me out the door, got me down, and choked me. After the fight, she said, "You have said enough to Jack Atkins and Ben Ferguson to hang you and Tom Dula if it was ever looked into." I replied, "You know you are as deep into it as I am." I also said that it was the truth that I had made the remark to Atkins and Ferguson but not that I had done the crime. I went off with her to the top of the hill. She then proposed to go back and make Mrs. Scott promise not to tell it. We went back, and Ann Melton enjoined on Mrs. Scott not to tell anything that had been said during our quarrel.

(The prisoner excepted.)

The Prisoner remarked to me one day that Ann Melton was jealous of me. I replied [that] I did not know how that

128

could be, as I never went into his company unless she put me in it for a blind.

In response to cross-examination: After we went off from Mrs. James Scott's, Ann Melton said to me she wanted to kill me ever since I had said that to Jack Atkins and Ben Ferguson. We had quarrelled that morning because she wanted me to milk the cows and get breakfast both. We had got off about one hundred yards when we turned back to Mrs. Scott's. Ann Melton went back a second time, but I could not distinguish the words she used. She said she was going back again to make Mrs. Scott promise not to tell anything that had taken place there. During the difficulty she had charged me with having a bad disease and also with having had improper intimacy with my brother. The latter charge was untrue.

MRS. JAMES SCOTT

Mrs. James Scott (recalled by the State) testified: Pauline Foster came to my house and a few minutes afterwards Ann Melton came.

(Seventh exception: Here, the witness was proceeding to give her version of the difficulty which occurred at her house between Pauline Foster and Mrs. Ann Melton when objection was made on the part of the prisoner, for the reasons set forth in the fourth exception, to wit: Dula was not present at the occurrence after the alleged murder. The objection was overruled.)

The witness resumed: Ann Melton came and ordered Pauline to go home, pushed her out of the chair, drew a stick over her, threw her down and choked her. She kept ordering her to go and used very abusive language to her. She also said Pauline had told Ben Ferguson enough to hang her ownself and that she had said she and Tom Dula had killed and put away Laura Foster and had also said, "Come out, Tom Dula, and let us kill some more." Pauline remarked, "I do say now, come out Tom Dula, and let us kill Ben Ferguson."

They went off together and both came back and Ann Melton enjoined on me to let it be a dying secret with me not to tell she said (that) she had started out that morning to take revenge and had commenced with her best friend. Ann afterwards came back by herself, appeared to be still mad. She said she would follow me to hell if I told it, and if it was told, she would know where it came from — as but four had heard it.

(The prisoner excepted.)

In response to cross-examination: Pauline said "it is the truth and you are as deep in the mud as I am in the mire." Ann replied, "You are a liar!" Ann threw up to Pauline having a disease. Pauline replied, "Yes, we all have it!" I have seen Pauline sitting in Dula's lap often, and [them] whispering together. Ann was always present on these occasions. I remember that Pauline and Dula came to my house together once. I have seen Ann Melton also sit in Dula's lap.

WASHINGTON ANDERSON

Washington Anderson testified: I was at James Melton's on Thursday night before the Friday Laura Foster disappeared. James Melton, Jonathan Gilbert, and Pauline Foster were there. Mrs. Ann Melton was not there. I stayed about two hours. I went by there next morning. Ann Melton was then on the bed sick. Her shoes were wet. I did not see her dress. The folks were eating breakfast.

Cross-examination: The shoes were women shoes and were by the bed. I could not swear whose they were. James Melton is a shoemaker. I knew the general character of the prisoner while in the Army. I was in the same company and regiment. His character was good as a soldier. I knew him as a truthful man and as a peaceable man while at home, and he was good for honesty.

I remember Pauline Foster meeting Dula one night near the road. I also remember her spending the night with him in the woods. I was along with them.

JOHN (JACK) ATKINS

John Atkins testified: I went after Thomas Dula into Tennessee about a month after the disappearance of Laura Foster. He said he had changed his name to Hall while in Watauga County, said that he did it for fun.

COL. [JAMES M.] ISBELL

Col. Isbell [recalled by the State] testified: I was at the grave at the time of its discovery. My father-in-law [David E. Horton] was with me. It [the discovery] was made as follows: Pauline Foster was arrested and, while in jail, gave substantially the same statement which she has made here today. In consequence of the disclosure made by her, she was taken out of jail. We went with her to the ridge, came to the log, saw where dirt had been removed. This was the spot where she stated she stopped following Ann Melton. After half an hour's search we found the grave seventy-five yards from this place. The earth had been carried away and the sod replaced. It escaped our observation until my companion's [Horton's] horse snorted and gave signs of smelling something. We then searched narrowly about the spot and by probing the ground discovered the grave. After taking out the earth, I saw the prints of what appeared to have been a mattock in the hard side of the grave. The flesh was off the face. The body had on a checked cotton dress [and] a dark-colored cloak or cape. There was a bundle of clothes laid on the head. There was also a small breast pin. I noticed in a former search we made about the Bates place, we found a rope around a dogwood tree seventy-five yards from the road in the bushes. We also saw another place where there were signs of a horse having been hitched; this was some two hundred yards from the dogwood. The horse had dunged twice. About fifteen steps off from this latter place we found a discolored spot of ground; the earth smelt offensive. Some broken bushes were lying on the ground near [by]. They had been disturbed when I saw them. The grave was not far from the path leading from Lotty Foster's house, but it was on a secluded, thickety ridge.

During the search we discovered a large mudhole near Francis Melton's which we intended to drag but it being late in the evening, put off until the next day. The next day we discovered signs of mud leading off from that direction toward the Yadkin River near Witherspoon's. We had not noticed these signs the day before. We dragged the hole but found nothing. No other female had disappeared from that neighborhood at that time except Laura Foster. No other person had gone off from the neighborhood except Thomas Dula.

In response to cross-examination: I think it was about five or six weeks after the disappearance of Laura Foster, before Pauline Foster left for Watauga. She was arrested twice. It was generally reported that Ann Melton indulged in illicit intercourse with others besides the prisoner.

I have assisted in employing counsel for the prosecution. I have no feeling of enmity against the accused. I am influenced solely by consideration of public good.

DR. GEORGE N. CARTER

Dr. George A. Carter (recalled by the State) testified: I have heard Pauline Foster examined heretofore; [I] also heard her evidence on this trial. Her evidence is substantially the same with some exceptions as to matters on which she was not questioned. I observed no conflict in her evidence upon the two occasions.

(Here the State rested its case. The foregoing witnesses were separated, with the exception of Col. Isbell and Dr. Carter. Mrs. Ann Melton was allowed to be in court during the examination.)

(The prisoner's witnesses were also separated.)

THOMAS FOSTER

Thomas Foster [recalled for prisoner] testified: I slept part of the night that Friday night at James Melton's with Pauline Foster. I have seen Pauline and Dula sitting in each other's lap.

J. W. WINKLER

J. W. Winkler [recalled for prisoner] testified: I was present when Pauline Foster was examined at a store in Elkville before a magistrate about this matter. After her examination, she remarked to a person there present, "I would swear a lie any time for Tom Dula, wouldn't you, George?"

MRS. MARY DULA

Mrs. Mary Dula testified as follows: I am the mother of the prisoner. He was twenty-two years of age on the 20th of June last [June 20, 1866]. His home was with me. Thomas was not at my house early in the morning of that Friday. I left the house after early breakfast that day and got back just before dinner [noon meal] hour. [I] found him lying on the bed. He ate no dinner and was there until sundown or thereabouts. While I was getting supper, he started away and stayed off about the barn. He came back to supper. He went to bed as usual. I heard him during the night making a little moan. I went to his bed. He had been complaining of chills. He was my sole remaining boy. I had lost two in the War. I leaned my face down and kissed him. I did not hear him go out that night and have no knowledge of his doing so. He was there in the morning until after breakfast.

In response to cross-examination: I did not say in the presence of Carson Gilbert or others that Friday that I did not know where my son Thomas was. I met them on the afternoon of that day near Lotty Foster's on the path between her house and mine. I had walked out to look after my cows. In reply to an inquiry made of me, I told them, "I did not know where Thomas was unless he had gone to muster." I did that at his request, as he said he was too unwell to go to the muster and did not want to be bothered by people making inquiries. The prisoner went out just at dark that evening and stayed about an hour. He went to bed that night before I did and took his clothes off as usual.

I have a grown daughter named Eliza, who lives with me. I left her home on the occasion of my leaving on that Friday morning. I have no recollection of hearing her say that Thomas had been away all day.

In response to direct examination [resumed]: On the path between my house and Lotty Foster's there was a very narrow place, steep and bad for cattle to pass. I don't know who worked it, but I noticed as I passed along on that Friday that it had been recently worked. It had been some two or three days before that, I had passed along it.

RUFUS HORTON

Rufus Horton testified that he was acquainted with the general character of Mrs. Mary Dula, the last witness, and that it was good for truth and honesty; he had never heard it doubted [that she was honest].

(Here the prisoner rested his case.)

(The State resumed its evidence.)

JESSE GILBERT

Jesse Gilbert testified: I saw Mrs. Mary Dula on that Friday evening [afternoon] as Carson and myself went by Lotty Foster's house.

(Here, the State proposed to offer as evidence the witness's version of what was said on that occasion to and by the witness Mrs. Dula with the view of contradicting her. This was objected to by the prisoner for the reason that this was a collateral matter sufficiently inquired into and that the State was precluded from further inquiry, being bound by the answer of the witness. The objection was overruled and the evidence was allowed by the Court.)

The witness then stated that Carson [Gilbert] called to Mrs. Dula and asked her where her son Tom was. She replied that she did not know; she hadn't seen him that day. [He was] gone to the muster, I expect.

(The prisoner excepted.)

This was about 3:00 p. m. We walked thirteen miles that evening [afternoon] by dark after seeing her.

MARTHA GILBERT

Martha Gilbert (recalled by the State) testified: Along where I saw the prisoner skelping the path the day I alluded to, it wasn't steep. The path was steep and broken further on towards Mrs. Dula's but not towards Lotty Foster's.

(Here the State closed its case and the prisoner resumed his evidence.)

135

Rufus Horton (recalled by the prisoner) testified: I know the general character of Jesse Gilbert. It is bad for stealing and lying.

(Here the prisoner closed his case.)

The prisoner's counsel **asked the Judge to charge** [the jury]:

1st — that circumstantial evidence, to authorize the jury to convict upon it, must be at least as strong as the positive and direct testimony of one credible witness.

2nd — that the circumstances proved must exclude every other hypothesis.

3rd — that the evidence must convince the jury of the prisoner's guilt beyond a reasonable doubt.

4th — that unless they are satisfied that there was a conspiracy between the prisoner and Ann Melton and that they acted in concert in the perpetration of the homicide, nothing that she said or did not in the presence of the prisoner is any evidence against the prisoner.

5th — that if they are satisfied that there was no confederacy between the prisoner and Ann Melton and that they acted in concert in the perpetration of the homicide, then nothing done or said by Ann Melton not in the presence of the prisoner would be evidence against the prisoner except acts done in futherance of the common design and declaration accompanying such acts.

The above instructions were given, as asked, in the charge of the Court to the jury. The jury, having returned a verdict of guilty against the prisoner, his counsel moved for *venico de novo* for the error in the Court in admitting the evidence excepted to on the trial. The rule was granted. A motion was then made in Arrest of Judgment on the following grounds:

1st — For a defect in the Record, stating the arraignment of the prisoner and Ann Melton was arraigned together, whereas the word *with* is used in the singular manner, thus showing but one of the accused had pleaded to the Judgment.

2nd — Objections to Bill of Indictment. It is not specified in the body of the bill that the offense is alleged to have been committed in the State of North Carolina. The name of the State appears only in the caption.

Motion in Arrest was overruled. The judgment of death was pronounced upon the prisoner, from which judgment he craved and obtained an appeal to the [State] Supreme Court. The appeal was allowed without security according to the act of the [General] Assembly, the prisoner being unable to give it [security].

There follows here a short summary of the brief of the State counsel, the arguments, cases cited as authority, etc. But this is treated so completely in the decision of the Supreme Court it is better excluded here.

Following is the text of Judge Buxton's ruling:

The prisoner being brought to bar of the court in the custody of the sheriff, motion in arrest of judgment. Overruled and judgment being produced by the solicitor and upon this, it is demanded of the said Thomas Dula if he hath any thing to say wherefore this court here ought not, upon the premises and verdict aforesaid to proceed to Judgment and execution against him, who nothing further saith than he has already said, whereupon all and singular the premises being seen and by the court here fully understood, it is considered by the court here that the said Thomas Dula be taken to the jail of Iredell County, whence he came, there to remain until the 9th day of November, 1866 and that on that day he be taken by sheriff of said County to the place of public execution of said county, between the hours of 10 o'clock a. m. and 4 o'clock p. m. and there hanged by the neck until he be dead. From which judgment the said Thomas Dula makes an appeal to the Supreme Court, and it appearing to the satisfaction of the Court here that the said Thomas Dula is insolvent, the said Thomas Dula is allowed to appeal without security.

And at Spring term, 1867 of our said Superior Court of Law being held for our said county of Iredell on the 7th Monday after the last Monday in February, 1867 [April 15] — the Honorable Robert B. Gelliam, Judge, present and presiding, the following Record was made:

State
vs
Thomas Dula
Ann Melton

Special venue of one hundred freeholders summoned for jury to appear on Wednesday morning of the Term at the hour of 10 o'clock.
Prisoners remanded to Jail.
Wednesday morning, April 17, 1867

State   Murder
vs
Thomas Dula &
Ann Melton

The prisoners Thomas Dula and Ann Melton again brought to the Bar of the Court upon motion this case was continued upon affidavit of Thomas Dula and set for hearing on Tuesday of the next term of the Court.
State vs Thomas Dula. In this case the defendant maketh oath that as he is advised and

believes he can not come safely to trial for the
want of the testimony of the following witnesses,
to wit: F. F. Hendricks, of Caldwell County;
Francis Farmer and Mary James of Watauga
County, all of whom are under supona [subpoena]
and absent without affiant's consent or procurement. Affiant further states that as he is
informed and believes all the above witnesses are
necessary and material for him in the trial of this
cause and that he expects to have the benefit of
the testimony of all of them at the next term of
this Court and that this affidavit is not made for
delay.

Thomas C. Dula

sworn and subscribed
before me this 17th of April
1867 — C. L. Summers, Clk.

The prisoners remanded to jail.

And at Fall Term, 1867 of our said Superior Court of Law
begun and held for our said County of Iredell on the 7th
Monday after the last Monday in August, 1867 [Oct. 14],
the Honorable Alexander Little, Judge was present and
presided. The following record was made:

State	Murder
vs	
Thomas Dula &	
Ann Melton	

The prisoners being brought to the bar of the court
by the Sheriff of our said county in whose custody
they are:

James Simmons, Lucinda Gordon, and J. [James]
W. M. Grason, witnesses for the State were called
and failed; therefore Judgment *ni si* was rendered
against them for the sum of Eighty Dollars each.

On motion this case was continued upon the
part of the State, upon the affidavit of Wilson
Foster for the want of testimony of James
Simmons, Lucinda Gordon, and J. W. M. Grason.

The following is the affidavit, to wit:

State	Murder	Superior Court of
vs		Law & Equity
Thomas Dula &		Fall Term, AD 1867
Ann Melton		

Wilson Foster maketh oath that the State is not
ready for the trial of this case for want of the
testimony of James W. M. Grason, James Simmons,
and Lucinda Gordon; that the said James W. M.
Grason and James Simmons are under recognizance
as witnesses in this case; that the materiality of
Lucinda Gordon as a witness was not known until
at Wilkes Superior Court and that a supone
[subpoena] was issued at once for said Lucinda
Gordon, but that Lucinda is unable to attend court
on account of sickness, to wit: Typhoid fever as
affiant is informed and believes; that the said J. W.
M. Grason is a citizen of the State of Tennessee
and is now attending the session of the Legislature
of Tennessee, of which body he is a member at this
time as affiant is informed and believes. That all
the said witnesses are material and necessary
witnesses to the State in the prosecution of this
case, and are absent without his consent or
procurement and that the State cannot come safely

to trial without their evidence and he expects the State to have the benefit of their testimony at the next term of his Court and this affidavit is not made for delay.

Subscribed and sworn before me
this 16th Oct., 1867
C. L. Summers, Clk.

his
Wilson X Foster
mark

State of North Carolina
Iredell County

Be it remembered that a Court of Oyer and Terminer was opened and held for the County of Iredell at the Court House in Statesville on the third Monday in January AD 1868 being the 20th day of said month in said year. The Honorable Wm. M. Shipp one of the judges in and for said State was present and presided as judge by virtue of the following commission to him directed:
State of North Carolina:
To the Honorable Wm. M. Shipp, greeting
The General Assembly by having vested in the governor the power to direct Court of Oyer and Terminer to be held for the speedy trial of "persons charged with capital felonies, crimes, misdemeanors, or any offenses against or in violation of the statute laws of the State or any violation or offense whatever of the criminal law of which the Superior Court at their regular terms have jurisdiction" and good cause having been shown why such court should be held in the County of Iredell, you are hereby nominated, appointed, and commissioned to hold such court

of Oyer and Terminer in said county at such early time as you may appoint. In witness whereof His Excellency Jonathan Worth, our governor — Captain General and commander in chief has hereunto set his hand and caused the great seal of the State to be affixed.

Done at the City of Raleigh this thirteenth day of December in the year of our Lord one thousand, eight-hundred and sixty-seven and in the ninety-second year of our Independence.

Jonathan Worth

By the governor
W. H. Bagby, private secretary

And at said term of court of Oyer and Terminer The following proceedings were had, to wit:

State	Murder
vs	
Thomas Dula &	
Ann Melton	

The prisoners being brought to the bar of the Court Whereupon the following order was made Ordered by the Court that the Sheriff of Iredell County summon a special venue of one hundred jurors to appear on Tuesday morning of the Term at the hour of 10 o'clock.

Prisoners remanded to jail. Court adjourned until Tuesday morning 10 o'clock.

(Tuesday morning, January 21, 1868, Tom Dula again filed an affidavit for severance.)

It is ordered by the Court that there be a severance in the case and the prisoners to be tried separately.

State   Murder   Pleas not guilty
  vs
Thomas Dula

The following jury to wit:

1. Albertus Cornelius
2. A. P. Sharpe
3. Samuel Dockery
4. Wm. Mears
5. James Lipe
6. Eli Bost
7. R. I. Davidson
8. Hiram Hastings
9. R. O. Sendler
10. Archibald Hoover
11. Willis Hooper
12. Dagwall Harkey

Being chosen, tried, and sworn to speak the truth of and concerning the premises upon their oath say that the said Thomas Dula is guilty of the felony and murder in manner and form as charged in the bill of indictment.

Motion in arrest of Judgment; motion overruled and judgment being prayed by the solicitor and upon this it is demanded of the said Thomas Dula if he have anything to say wherefore the court here ought to proceed and verdict aforesaid to proceed to judgment and execution against him, who nothing further saith than he has already said. Whereupon all and singular the prisoner being seen and by the Court here that the said Thomas Dula be taken to the Jail of Iredell County whence he came, there to remain until the 14th day of February, 1868 and that on that day he be taken by the Sheriff of said County to the place of public execution of said county between the hours of 10 o'clock am and 4 o'clock pm, and there hanged by the neck until he be dead: From the said Judgment the said Thomas Dula prayed an appeal to the Supreme Court, and it appearing to the satisfaction of the Court here that the said Thomas Dula is insolvent the said Thomas Dula is allowed to appeal without security.

The prisoners remanded to jail.

The following is the statement of the case made out by the Honorable Wm. M. Shipp Judge of our said Court to wit:

This was an indictment for murder, tried at a court of Oyer & Terminer for Iredell County. The indictment charged the prisoner Thomas Dula as principal in the murder of one Laura Foster of Wilkes County, and Ann Melton as accessory before the fact. The State relied upon circumstantial testimony to prove the homicide and upon the declarations and acts of Ann Melton in furtherance of an alleged agreement between the prisoner and the said Ann Melton, to commit the homicide. In order to establish the agreement between the parties it was in evidence to the court alone that Laura Foster was at home, at her father's house on Thursday night, the 24th day of May, 1866; that on Friday morning she was gone; that a mare tied in the yard was likewise gone. She [Laura] was seen early Friday morning riding the mare which belonged to her father, about a mile from home, going in the direction of a place known as the Bates Place. She was not seen by any witness after that time. A body was subsequently found near the Bates Place, buried in a rude manner in a remote place in a thicket of Laurel. This body was identified by her father and several other witnesses who swore that they knew it from the clothes and from the teeth, and the hair. The physician who examined the body swore that there was a wound on the left side near the heart, piercing through the dress [which] was found upon her, and into the cavity of her body. It was in evidence by the father of Laura Foster that the prisoner had visited her frequently before the alleged homicide that he had been seen in bed with her on one or two occasions. It was in evidence by the father that she had sores upon her person and that she had been taking medicine. It was in evidence by a physician that Thomas Dula had said to him in March, 1866, that he had a venereal disease called syphilis and that he had contracted that disease from Laura Foster. The physician treated him for that disease; he stated that the disease was in its primary state. It was in evidence by another person that the prisoner told him previous to the alleged homicide that he had this disease and that he intended to put the one through who give it to him. It was in evidence that the prisoner was at the house of the deceased on the Saturday previous to her death, that he was there on the Wednesday previous to that time, and that on both occasions he had private conversation with her. It was testified to that he was seen Friday morning, the same day on which the deceased left home, near her father's house, travelling on a road parallel to the one on which the girl was going. This road led among other places to the Bates Place, and was nearer than the one on which the girl was travelling. It was in evidence that the prisoner went to the house of Ann Melton on that Friday morning, found her in bed, and leant over and had a whisper conversation with her. It was in evidence that the prisoner on Thursday was at the house of Ann Melton, that he sent a man for a quart of liquor, that on the same day he went to the mother of Ann Melton and borrowed a mattock; he was seen with the same mattock a few hundred yards from where the grave was found on the same evening. It was in evidence that the quart of liquor was brought by the messenger to Ann Melton's house in the absence of the prisoner. It was in evidence by the sister and mother of Ann Melton that she came to their house [where the prisoner had borrowed the mattock] and that she requested a little girl to go down to the prisoner's mother's and tell him to come up and get his liquor, but not to tell him if his sister, Eliza, was there but to tread on his toes or to pinch him and tell him mother wanted to see him. The girl went down and did not find him. He afterwards came and he and Ann Melton had a private conversation and each went off in opposite directions. It was in evidence that Ann Melton did not return home on Thursday night but that she came home on Friday morning before day with her dress and shoes wet. She remained in bed the greater part of the day on Friday. There was evidence that Ann Melton and the prisoner had been on most intimate terms for a number of years and that an adulterous intercourse had been kept up between them and that he visited the house daily. It was also in evidence that Ann Melton had a sore mouth and that she had taken medicine for it previous to the death of Laura Foster. It was further proved that Thomas Dula came to Ann Melton's house on Thursday morning and said that he had met Ann Melton on the ridge not far from the house, shortly before that time and that she told him where to get some alum and a canteen; upon this testimony, it was insisted on the part of the state that there was sufficient evidence of an agreement between the prisoner and Ann Melton to commit the alleged homicide to authorize the declations [declarations], admissions, and acts of hers in furtherance of said agreement, to be given in evidence. The hypothesis on the part of the State was that the grave was dug on Thursday or Thursday night, that the deceased was killed on Friday or Friday night, that the motive for the perpetration of the murder was the resentment caused by the fact that the prisoner had caught a disgusting venereal disease from the deceased and had communicated it to his paramour, Ann Melton. The State offered to prove declarations, admissions, etc. of Ann Melton. This testimony was objected to by the prisoner, but the Court being of the opinion that the evidence stated above, which was testified to by various witnesses, was true and that it established an agreement overruled an agreement (,) overruled the objection [sic]. The Court instructed the jury that the evidence offered to the Court of the acts, etc. of Ann Melton were admitted by the Court for its information as to whether there was an agreement between her and the prisoner to commit the homicide but that this opinion of the Court was to have no weight with them when they came to decide upon the prisoner's guilt or innocence upon all the evidence. Prisoner excepts. Various declarations of Ann Melton previous to the alledged [sic] murder threatening vengeance against Laura Foster were proved. Declarations of hers on Thursday previous to the day on which she was killed stating that she had contracted a venereal disease from the prisoner and that he had got it from Laura Foster and that she intended to have her revenge or that she intended to kill her or have her killed were proved by a witness. There was evidence of a secret and private conference between them, prisoner and Ann Melton on Thursday morning on the ridge between Ann Melton's and her mother's. The Canteen in which the liquor had been brought to her house by the messenger on Thursday was found by a witness on Friday morning under a tree where Ann Melton told her it was. There was a very small quantity of liquor left in the canteen. It was in evidence to the Jury that the prisoner said he had received the canteen of liquor by a witness who saw him that evening [afternoon] on his way up the River. There was mass of circumstantial testimony in evidence before the jury tending to show the prisoner's connection with the alleged homicide. All the evidence was submitted to the jury under a charge from the Court to which no exception was taken. Among other witnesses, Mrs. Scott was examined who swore that she saw Laura Foster on Friday morning riding on her father's mare with a bundle of clothes travelling in the direction of the place called Bates place, that Laura as she was passing told witness that she was going to the Bates place. It was objected to by the prisoner, that the witness should state the declarations of Laura Foster. The Court overruled the objection. The prisoner excepted. Afterwards in the progress of the argument the solicitor on the part of the State stated that in asmuch as this testimony was objected to on the part of the prisoner, he withdrew it and asked the Court and Jury so to consider it. The prisoner's counsel, in reply to the argument of the solicitor, complained of the course on the part of the prosecution in asmuch as the evidence had been heard by the Jury. The Court in summing up the evidence did not notice the declarations of Laura Foster and treated them as withdrawn. Another witness was examined on the part of the State, a white woman by the name of Eliza Anderson. In the course of the crossexamination, prisoner's counsel proposed to ask witness if she was related to John Anderson — John Anderson was a man of color. The object as stated was to disparage or discredit her. Upon objection, the question was ruled out. Prisoner excepted. The Jury found the defendant guilty. Motion for a new trial. Motion refused. Motion in arrest of Judgment. Motion overruled. Judgment being pronounced, defendant prayed an appeal to the Supreme Court, which was granted.

W. M. Shipp JSCSE

(C. S. Summers, the Clerk of Superior Court of Iredell County sent a record to the Supreme Court made from Judge Buxton's case, tried in 1866. He received a complaint back from the Supreme Court and wrote the above summary (with Judge Shipp's advice, surely) from Judge Shipp's trial. Summers' letter of apology is below.)

149

Clerk Supreme Court

Dear Sir. Yours for a more perfect transcript of the record in the case of State vs. Dula came to hand on the 5th Inst. I herewith send you the record amended as I understand from your writ and (JMC) attorney. I hope it will be all right. The former record was made from and by Judge Baxter's case on the former trial. I thought it covered all the ground in the case.

Respectfully yours etc.

C. S. Summers, CSC

There was no exception to the charge of the Court to the Jury — but many exceptions to the admissibility of the evidence offered and allowed. As this [is] is a case of circumstantial evidence the presiding Judge has thought [it] proper to set forth all the evidence, especially since the counsel assigned by the Court to defend the prisoner have entrusted to the Judge the duty of making up the case. The exceptions are carefully noted.

The Unidentified Transcript

The following transcript was among some miscellaneous Wilkes County criminal papers in the State Archives. It contains notes taken during Pauline Foster's testimony, but the time and the place are not indicated. The transcript starts abruptly and breaks off in the middle of a sentence. The original notes are jotted down in fragments with few or no punctuation marks other than dashes. I have tried to make statements of the fragments, generally, and have occasionally added a word or words in brackets to complete the sense of a statement.

Ann Pauline Foster — lived and worked at Mr. Melton — went there last March this year — related to Ann Melton — came from Watauga — age 21 — came to see her grandfather & saw Ann Melton and James. They offered her 21 dollars to work thru this summer — never saw Dula until she went to Dula's [Melton's?] house there the day she went. He was there every day or every night. Came when Melton was away if possible. If not came when he was there. Would stay all night and sleep with Ann — 3 beds in the house. Pauline in one, Ann in another & Dula pretend to sleep with M in another. Quarrel between Dula and Thomas Foster. Ann and Tom sometimes fell out. Melton never slept with wife. Dula never slept with Ann frequently while Melton was there. Dula never slept with witness nor Melton. Dula would romp with witness, would say he did it to make people to think [so people would not think] he came to see Ann — would always devote himself to Ann when by themselves. Ann had great influence over Dula. She and Dula were going over to beat Mr. Griffin. Never heard her speak to him about Laura Foster — had heard her quarrel with him about Caroline Barnes. Ann told her [Pauline] she was diseased a short time before [a few days] she threatened Laura. She was very angry. On Thursday morning she told her Dula had given her the disease and that Laura gave it to him. She would fool Melton [who had it] but would have her revenge. She would have to do with Melton and make him think he gave it to her. She said that she was going to kill Laura Foster and if I [witness] should leave that place that day or talk about [it] with anybody she would kill me — did not call Dula's name said she would [go] to her mothers — and take the liquor to Dula — [Carson Dula returned about 10 o'clock with liquor] — when she [Pauline] returned from the field the liquor was there. Ann took the canteen and left with it. Took a drink before she left — said it was for Dula. That morning two hours after Dula and Carson Dula left, Ann came back. Dula and she would have probably met. Ann did not come back until about an hour before day next morning. Shoes and tail of her dress were wet. She pulled off [shoes and dress] and got in bed. Said her and her mother and Dula had laid out that night and drunk that canteen of liquor. Melton was afraid to ask her any questions about anything. Ann boasted that she could make Dula do anything, that she always kept everybody about her under her [control]. Ann was scarcely up when witness came back from field. Wilson Foster came at night, then Tom [Foster], then Washington Anderson, then Will Holder. Gilbert was there working. Witness said to Tom Foster, "When have you seen Dula?" He said, "He saw him that evening." Wilson Foster said he reckoned they [Laura and Tom] had got married and gone off with his mare. Ann got up late before bedtime and put on her clothes. Tom Foster and witness sat up and talked until past midnight. Didn't miss Ann at all. Saturday morning she said "she'd done what she said." Said she got up in the night and Pauline and Tom [Foster] knew nothing about it. On Saturday or Sunday she said she had killed Laura

Foster. [She] commenced cussing about that disease. After seeing Dula Thursday morning I didn't see him any more until Friday morning. Was starting out to work. Came back to get her milk vessels. Dula and Ann were talking secretly when she entered the house. Ann was lying on the bed. Didn't see Dula [after that] until Saturday morning tolerably early. Wanted James to fix shoes or fiddle. Dula and Ann talked a long time. Witness told she thought he and Laura Foster had run off. Dula laughed and said "what use do you suppose I would have for Laura Foster?" That night Dula returned and brought his fiddle, played it until bedtime. Played witness to sleep. Came every day or night until he went to Tennessee. Frequently mentioned report to Dula that he had killed Laura Foster. He would laugh and say they would have to prove it and he would whip them besides. The night he ran way he came [four weeks after the murder]. Ann pulled a board off inside the wall, punched the dirt out, put her knife under her pillow, drew a nail outside, put a string around her wrist for Dula to pull. Said she would fight for Dula if they arrested him. James Melton learned Dula was about to be arrested and told him in witness's presence. Dula cussed the Hendrickses about it. About 1:20 o'clock, Dula went off after a while. This was Sunday. Ann said he came back next morning and then went up to Hendricks'. He came back about dark [Ann had fixed the knife, string, etc.] from towards Hendricks's. Hadn't much to say. Appeared as if his feelings were hurt. Said he was going home that night. Said wouldn't stay, but changed his mind and lay down on bed. Dula then cried. Ann went out in the yard. Witness and Dula went out in the yard to Ann. Dula denied it [the murder]. Said he was going to leave. Would come back Christmas for his mother and would take Ann with him. Had his arms around Ann. Both crying. Dula told them both good-by. Heard him crying. Ann cried so that Melton asked her what was the matter. She said "Dula was leaving." Dula had a Bowie knife. Carried it in a pocket made in his coat. Description of knife. About three weeks afterwards witness went to Watauga with her brother. Taylor Land heard conversation with Ann about it [leaving]. Ann was not milking. Followed Pauline some distance to get her back. Dula had been brought back and put in jail before she left. Ann Melton and Sam Foster came to Watauga after witness. She [Pauline] came [back] with her. Ann told Pauline that they were talking about arresting her [Pauline] and induced her to come back. Ann frequently sent things to Dula. About 3 weeks after Pauline came back from Watauga, Ann, crying, said, "Poor Dula. I wonder if he will be hung. Are you a friend of Dula? I am. Are you a friend of mine. I want to show you Laura Foster's grave. They have pretty well quit hunting for it. I want to see whether it looks suspicious." If so she would carry body to cabbage patch soon next morning and work over. Then changed her notion and said "no that won't do. I will take her over and put her in the big [Several words are obscure here]. Would cut her up and put her in a bag and carry her. They started to the grave. Went up ridge road to Lotty Foster's, then off through an old field, then crossed Reedy Branch, then mounted another ridge and came to a pine log, where the dirt was apparently rooted up by hogs. Ann said the grave was up further between trees [and] ivy bushes. Covered up the ground with leaves to prevent suspicion. Pauline refused to go further. Ann wanted to go to the grave, and cussed witness terribly until they got to the creek [branch]. Told witness at the creek that if she ever told this, she [Ann] would put witness where Laura Foster was. When they got near home, [Ann] pretended it was a dream. About a week afterwards, John [Jack] Adkins and Ben Ferguson came to Melton's. All sitting there talking. Ben said he believed witness helped kill Laura Foster and ran to Watauga on account of it. Witness said, "Yes, Tom and I did kill Laura," squeezing Adkin's hand and laughing at him. Ann said, "You have said enough to hang you and Dula both, but you said it in a joke." Then joke with a rope, etc. [The transcript ends abruptly here.]

State of N. C.
Iredell County

Be it remembered that a Superior Court of Law was opened held for the county of Iredell at the court house in Statesville on the 7th Monday after the last Monday in February AD 1868 it being the 13 day of April in said year. The Honorable Anderson Mitchell one of the judges in and for said state present and presiding.

The following to wit appears:

State	Murder
vs	
Thomas Dula	

It is ordered by the Court that the prisoner Thomas Dula be brought to the bar of the Court by the Sheriff of Iredell County. The prisoner Thomas Dula being brought to the bar, of the Court, by the sheriff of Iredell County in whose custody he is.

It being by the solicitor for the State that the Court pass judgment upon the prisoner and upon this it is demanded of the said Thomas Dula, if he hath anything to say wherefore the Court here ought not upon the premises and verdict aforesaid to proceed to judgment and Execution against him. Whereupon all and singular the premises being seen and by the Court here being fully understood it is considered by the Court here that the said Thomas Dula be taken to the Jail of Iredell County whence [he] came, there to remain until Friday, the 1st day of May AD 1868, and that on that date he be taken by the Sheriff of said county to the place of public Execution of said county between the hours of 12 o'clock [noon] and four P. M. and there be hanged by the neck until he be dead. It appearing to the satisfaction of the Court here that the prisoner Thomas Dula is unable to pay the cost of this prosecution It is therefore considered and adjudged by the Court here. That the County of Wilkes pay the costs of this prosecution.

	Bill costs in Wilkes County
State	
vs	
Thomas Dula	to wit

2 indictments & certificates	2.40
4 orders	1.20
2 Capias's (es)	2.25

11 Subpoenas		2.37½ 23.37½
7 Seals		2.00
17 Probates		2.53
21 Recogniances [recognizances]		6.30
1 Affidavit		.30
Transcript seal		3.37
George N. Carter	State witness	15.30
C. C. Jones	,, ,,	7.80
J. M. Isbell	,, ,,	7.80
Calvin Carlton	,, ,,	8.00
Wilson Foster	,, ,,	8.40
James Melton	,, ,,	12.04
Thomas Foster	,, ,,	4.80
H. Kendall	,, ,,	4.74
Ben Ferguson	,, ,,	4.38
Carson Dula	,, ,,	4.80
Bennett Walsh	,, ,,	12.30
G. W. Anderson	,, ,,	1.92
Wilson Foster	,, ,,	5.10
James Foster	,, ,,	5.10
Tempy Pilkerton	,, ,,	3.30
J. C. Horton	,, ,,	7.10
J. W. Winkler	Def. Wit.	<u>5.10</u>
		118.18
W. H. Witherspoon	D. S.	2.70
P. Tomlinson	D. S.	1.50
W. White	D. S.	8.00
Thomas McNeil	Guard	2.10
B. F. McNeil	,,	2.16
Poindexter Jones		1.96
Lee Saintclair	Guard	2.16
E. Cranor	Jailer	<u>100.95</u>
		103.11
Costs in Iredell Superior Court		
Entering	C. L. S. Clk	.60

3 Continuances	C. L. S. Clk	.90
49 Subpoenas	State " "	7.35
45 Seals	" "	11.25
Postage on same	" "	.36
2 Motions in arrest of Judgment		.60
2 " for new Trial	"	.60
3 Orders	"	.90
2 Appeals	"	1.20
35 Recognizances	"	7.00
3 Transcripts & Postage Superior Court Clk.		8.57
Judgment and bill	"	1.10
1 Affidavit	"	.20
G. W. Brown Clk 4 Subpoenas		.60
2 Seals		.50
		1,111

Sheriff Wm. F. Wasson summoning

3 special Venue 100 each	60.00
Executing subpoenas	1.50
Sheriff Wasson 2 Juries counted (?)	.20
" " Executing prisoner	10.00
	71.70

D. S. W. T. Watts Executing and Subp.	.30
Sheriff John Horton	.30
Sheriff R. R. Call	6.30
D. S. Ed Brown	1.20
" J. A. Wakefield	.30
" J. L. Laxton	1.80
" R. D. Hall	.60
Sheriff W. G. Hix	.60
" " " " Conveying prisoner to Iredell	8.00
" 1 guard	4.00
D. S. W. H. Witherspoon	24.30
	47.70

State Witnesses

Franklin West   (to use Miller and Vanfelt) 14.50

R. D. Hall	(to use Templeton & McLean)		8.30
J. G. Melton	,,	,,	7.80
Jos Howard col	,,	,,	8.10
A. P. Scott	,,	,,	13.40
C. Dula	,,	,,	8.10
Thos. M. Dula	,,	,,	7.70
W. C. Dula	,,	,,	8.10
J. H. Jones	,,	,,	8.10
Dr. G. N. Carter	,,	,,	13.70
L. B. Welch	,,	,,	<u>8.20</u>
			91.70
Ben Ferguson (to use Carlton & Morrison)			7.60
James Scott	,,	,,	9.45
R. D. Hall	,,	,,	8.05
J. G. Melton	,,	,,	9.55
B. H. Welch	,,	,,	9.55
M. C. Hendricks	,,	,,	10.50
Carson Dula	,,	,,	9.55
Calvin Carlton	,,	,,	9.65
Elizabeth Scott	,,	,,	9.65
B. D. Ferguson	,,	,,	9.65
John Adkins	,,	,,	9.15
J. M. Isbell	,,	,,	9.15
R. D. Horton	,,	,,	9.15
G. N. Carter	,,	,,	9.15
Wilson Foster	,,	,,	9.65
Hezekiah Kendall	,,	,,	9.45
J. W. Winkler	,,	,,	5.70
Eliza Anderson	,,	,,	9.45
Martha Gilbert	,,	,,	9.25
J. P. Hoffman	,,	,,	9.90
Pauline Foster	,,	,,	14.65
Lotty Foster	,,	,,	9.25
Samuel Foster	,,	,,	9.25
Tempe Pilkerton	,,	,,	9.25

Thomas Foster	,,	,,	9.25
Celia Scott	,,	,,	9.45
G. W. Anderson	,,	,,	9.45
			244.55
C. P. Jones			27.70
G. N. Carter			13.60
D. E. Horton			21.30
Angeline Scott			6.60
G. H. Brown			7.15
			76.35
W. H. Witherspoon			20.20
Martha Foster (to use W. H. Witherspoon)			13.20
Richard Swanson	,,	,,	14.10
Lucinda Witherspoon	,,	,,	14.40
Theodocia ,,	,,	,,	13.40
			76.00
Phenias Horton			13.40
G. W. Hendricks (to use Phenias Horton)			11.60
Lydney Welch	,,	,,	14.30
John Hoffman	,,	,,	21.15
J. M. Isbell	,,	,,	27.30
D. P. Adkins	,,	,,	30.70
Thomas Hall	,,	,,	14.10
Wm. Adkins	,,	,,	14.30
George Triplett	,,	,,	22.20
Gay Hendricks	,,	,,	30.30
Leeander Hendricks	,,	,,	20.95
Elizabeth Scott	,,	,,	30.75
R. D. Hall	,,	,,	20.50
Cynthia Dula	,,	,,	14.10
Micajah Hendricks	,,	,,	31.25
Samuel Foster	,,	,,	19.50
Lotty Foster	,,	,,	20.20
Tiny Foster	,,	,,	20.20
Thomas M. Dula	,,	,,	19.70

B. D. Ferguson	,,	,,	13.60
Wilson Foster	,,	,,	29.30
James Foster	,,	,,	29.30
Alfred Witherspoon Col	,,	,,	13.60
Jesse Gilbert	,,	,,	14.10
Drewry Adkins	,,	,,	4.53
J. H. Jones	,,	,,	21.10
Celia Scott	,,	,,	20.90
B. H. Welch	,,	,,	30.90
C. Carlton	,,	,,	28.80
W. German	,,	,,	27.30
Beckia Gilbert	,,	,,	14.10
Rufus D. Horton	,,	,,	13.40
Rebecca Anderson	,,	,,	13.70
James Anderson	,,	,,	13.70
Eliza Anderson	,,	,,	19.90
G. W. Anderson	,,	,,	20.80
T. E. Witherspoon	,,	,,	5.60
H. Kendall	,,	,,	6.40
Alexander Melton	,,	,,	6.80
J. H. Adkins	,,	,,	9.10
J. G. Melton	,,	,,	6.60
Martha Foster	,,	,,	6.20
C. Dula	,,	,,	6.50
Martha Gilbert	,,	,,	6.40
Jos. Howard Col	,,	,,	14.20
James C. Horton	,,	,,	13.10

806.42

C. L. Summers this Transcript
24 copy sheets $2.40   1 seal   2.65
$1924.10
J. W. Winkler Debts credit   5.30
$1918.80

State of North Carolina
Iredell County

C. L. Summers Clerk

Superior Court for the County of Iredell do testify that the foregoing contains a full and perfect transcript of State cost in the case the State against Thomas Dula.

In testimony whereof I hereunto subscribe my name and affix the seal of said court in Statesville this 19th day of June 1868.

C. L. Summers Clk.

RULINGS OF THE STATE SUPREME COURT

State v. Thomas Dula.
(First ruling by N. C. Supreme Court)

1. To the rule requiring testimony to be subjected to the *tests* of "an oath" and "cross examination" there are exceptions, arising from necessity. One of these consists of declarations, which are part of the *res gestae.*
2. This exception embraces only such declarations as give character to an act; therefore, when the deceased was met a few miles from the place where she was murdered, going in the direction of that place, *Held* that her declarations, in a conversation with the witness, as to where the prisoner was and that she expected to meet him at the place whither she was going, were not admissible against him.
3. What facts amount to an agreement to commit a crime between the prisoner and one charged as accessory, so as to render competent the acts and declarations of the alleged accessory, is a question of law, and the decision of the court below upon it is subject to review in the Supreme Court.

4. So, whether there is any evidence of a common design. But whether the evidence proves the fact of common design, whether the witnesses are worthy of credit, and in case of conflict, what witnesses should be believed by the Judge, are questions of fact for him to decide, and are not liable to review.

(*State v. George*, 29 N. C., 321, and *State v. Andrew, ante,* p. 205, cited and approved.)

Murder, tried before *Buxton, J.,* at Fall Term, 1866, of the Superior Court of Iredell.

The prisoner was indicted as principal, and one Ann Melton as accessory before the fact, in the murder of one Laura Foster, in Wilkes County in May, 1866. The bill was found at Fall Term, 1866, of Wilkes Superior Court, and upon affidavit, removed to Iredell. The prisoner and Ann Melton were arraigned together, but, upon motion of the counsel for the former, there was a severance, and he put upon his trial alone.

The case, as made out by his Honor, contained a statement of all the evidence, and was quite voluminous. There were several exceptions by the prisoner on account of the admission of improper testimony. The opinion of this court makes it unnecessary to state them all, or to detail the evidence.

The body of the deceased was found a few weeks after she disappeared near a locality called "the Bates place," and was recognized. There were plain indications that the deceased had been murdered; and the testimony relied on to prove the guilt of the prisoner was circumstantial.

One Betsey Scott testified that she saw the deceased the morning of the day she was missing; "she was riding her father's mare, bareback, with a bundle of clothes in her lap," etc. It was then proposed to prove by the witness that in a conversation that ensued between her and the deceased, the latter said she was on her way to the Bates place; that the prisoner had returned just before day, was going another way, and she expected to meet him at the Bates place. The prisoner objected to the declarations, as not being a part of the *res gestae*; bu the testimony was admitted.

The other exceptions were principally to the admission of evidence of acts and declarations of Ann Melton. The prisoner contended that such evidence should not go to the jury, unless a common design between him and Ann Melton had first been established. His Honor overruled the exceptions, and the testimony was admitted.

Verdict of Guilty; Rule for a new trial; Rule discharged; Motion in arrest of judgment; Motion overruled; Judgment of Death, and Appeal.

Attorney General and *Boyden*, for the State.
Vance, for the prisoner.

Pearson, C. J. The case discloses a most horrible murder, and the public interest demands that the perpetrator of the crime should suffer death; but the public interest also demands that the prisoner, even if he be guilty, shall not be convicted, unless his guilt can be proved according to the law of the land.

The conversation between Mrs. Scott and the deceased ought not to have been admitted as evidence. At all events, no part of it except that the deceased said she was going to the Bates place. How what the deceased said in regard to the prisoner's having come just before day, and where he was, and that she expected to meet him, can in any sense be considered a part of the acts of the deceased — being on her father's mare, bare back, with a bundle of clothes in her lap, and coming from her father's past A. Scott's house, when the witness met her in the road — we are unable to perceive. The law requires all testimony, which is given to the jury, to be subjected to *two tests of its truth*: 1st. It must have the sanction of an oath. 2nd. There must be an opportunity of cross-examination. *Dying declarations* form an exception, and another exception is allowed when declarations constitute a part of the act, or *res gestae*. Acts frequently consist not only of an action or thing being done, but of words showing the nature and quality of the thing. In such cases, when the action or thing being done is offered in evidence, as a matter of course the words which form a part of it must also be received in evidence; as if one seizes another by the arm, saying, I arrest you under a State's warrant, these words are just as much a part of the act done as the action of taking him by the arm.

In this case the conversation between Mrs. Scott and the deceased, although it occurred at the time of the action or thing being done, to wit, her being in the road on her father's mare, bare back, cannot, in any point of view, be considered a part of the act. It was entirely accidental, and consisted simply of answers to inquiries which the curiosity of Mrs. Scott induced her to make. These answers may have been true, or they may have been false, but they were not verified by "*the tests*" which the law of evidence requires, and it was error to admit them as evidence against the prisoner.

As the case must go back for another trial, we do not feel at liberty to enter into an expression of opinion in regard to the other matters of exception. But we see from the case sent that his Honor fell into the error, for which a *venire de nova* is awarded at this term in *State v. Andrew*. That is, without stating distinctly how he decided the facts, preliminary to the admission of the acts and declarations of Ann Melton in furtherance of a common purpose to murder the deceased, upon the evidence offered to *the court* to establish these preliminary facts he allows the evidence to the jury, and instructs them that if they are not satisfied of the existence of a conspiracy between the prisoner and Ann Melton to effect the murder of the deceased, in that case they are to give to the acts and declarations of Ann Melton, which had been admitted as evidence to them no weight, and are not to be influenced by them. What facts amount to such an agreement between the prisoner and Ann Melton, to aid and assist each other in effecting the murder of the deceased, as to make her acts and declarations in furtherance of the common purpose evidence against him, is a question of law, and the decision in the court below may be reviewed in this court; so, what evidence the Judge should allow to be offered to him to establish these facts, is a question of law; so, whether there be *any evidence* tending to show the existence of such an agreement is a question of law. But whether the evidence, if true, proves these facts, and whether the witness giving testimony to *the court* touching the facts are entitled to credit or not, and, in case of a conflict of testimony, which witness should be believed by the court, are questions of fact to be decided by the Judge, and his decision cannot be reviewed in this court. See *State v. George*, 29 N. C., 321, and *State v. Andrew*, decided at this term, *ante*, p. 205, where the subject is fully explained. The remarks made in that case are applicable to this, not excepting what is said in reference to the prolixity of cases made up for this court.

In speaking of the connection necessary to be found between the prisoner and Ann Melton as preliminary to this admissibility of her acts and declarations, in furtherance of the common purpose, as evidence against him, I have used the word *"agreement"* to aid and assist each other to effect the death, in preference to the word *conspiracy*; for, although they have the same meaning, yet the latter is apt to lead to a confusion of ideas. If parties are indicted for a conspiracy to murder or do some other unlawful act, in that case the issue joined on the plea of *not guilty* is the fact of the conspiracy; the endeavor to prove it must, of course, be

167

given to the jury and passed upon by them. Otherwise, where the indictment is for the murder or other act, and the fact of an agreement is to aid and assist is only preliminary to the admissibility of the acts and declarations of one against the other.

Per Curiam.   *Venire de novo.*
Cited: State v. Dula, post 440; Devries v. Phillips, 63 N. C., 208.

The State v. Thomas Dula
(Ruling on second trial by N. C. Supreme Court)

1. Where there is any evidence of an agreement between two or more to compass the death of a third person, the decision of the court below that such evidence is *sufficient* to establish the agreement, (preliminary to the admission of the acts, etc., of one of such persons as evidence against the other), cannot be reviewed in the Supreme Court.
2. Although in investigating the preliminary question as to the agreement, evidence of the naked declarations of one of the parties is not competent; yet if such declarations make part of the act charged in the indictment, it is otherwise.
3. In order to support an exception to the exclusion of certain testimony, such testimony must appear to have been relevant.
4. What one says *in via*, as to the place to which he is going, is competent evidence to establish the truth of what he says.
5. It is no ground for an arrest of judgment that the name of the State is omitted in the body of the indictment; or that the memorandum of the pleas of two defendants is prefaced by the word "saith."

(*State v. Dula, ante* 211, and *State v. Lane*, 26 N. C., 113,
cited and approved.)

Murder, tried at a Court of Oyer and Terminer for Iredell,
upon the third Monday of January 1868, before *Shipp, J.*

The prisoner was charged as principal in the murder of one
Laura Foster, in Wilkes County, in January 1866; one Ann
Melton being charged in the same indictment as accessory
before the fact, but not being upon trial, in consequence of
an affidavit made by the prisoner.

The State relied upon circumstantial testimony, and upon
the acts and declarations of Ann Melton in furtherance of an
alleged agreement between her and the prisoner to commit
the homicide. To establish the agreement evidence was given
to the court that the deceased was at home, at her father's,
on Thursday night the 24th of January, but on the next
morning was gone, as was also a mare that had been tied in
the yard. Early on Friday she was seen upon the mare, about
a mile from home, going in the direction of "the Bates
place." She was not seen alive after that, but subsequently
her body was found rudely buried in a laurel thicket near
that place, and there was a wound upon her left side piercing
the cavity of the body. There was evidence that the prisoner
was in the habit of criminal intercourse with both the
deceased and Ann Melton; that some short while before he
had contracted a disease from the deceased and had
communicated it to Ann Melton, that he had threatened to
"put through" whoever had given it to him; that he had been
with the deceased at her home on the Sunday and Monday
before she disappeared, and there had private conversations
with her; that on Thursday and Friday he had had private
interviews with Ann Melton at her home, and on a ridge near
her home; that he had sent for liquor in a canteen when at
her house on Thursday, which was brought there in his
absence; whereupon, Ann Melton had sent for him by a little

girl, in a secret and singular manner, to come and get it, but her messenger did not find him; that afterwards he had come to her mother's house, and after a private conversation between them, he and Ann went off in opposite directions; that during the same day he had been at Ann Melton's house, saying, he had met her upon a ridge near by, and that she had told him where to get the canteen and some alum; that he had borrowed a mattock during the day from her mother and was seen with it near "the Bates place"; that on Friday morning he was seen travelling in the direction of "the Bates place," by a road which ran parallel with that by which Laura Foster was seen going; that Ann Melton, after leaving her mother's, did not return to her own house until Friday morning, when her shoes and dress were wet, and she retired to bed, remaining there most of the day; after she had gone to bed the prisoner came there, leaned over her, and had a whispered conversation with her.

The hypothesis of the State was that the grave was dug on Thursday or Thursday night, and the deceased killed on Friday or Friday night; and that the motive was the communication of the disease.

On motion of the State, the court held that the above circumstances were sufficient to authorize the introduction of Ann Melton's acts and declarations in furtherance of the common design; cautioning the jury at the same time that this decision was to have no weight with them as to the prisoner's guilt or innocence.

To this decision the prisoner excepted; as he did specially to the Court's hearing evidence, whilst taking information upon that point, as to the message sent by the little girl.

Evidence was admitted that Laura Foster had said to a witness, whilst riding in the direction of the Bates' place, that she was going to that place. To this the prisoner had excepted, and at a subsequent stage of the trial the State agreed that it should not be considered as in evidence; and the court thereupon, in charging the jury, told them not to regard it. The prisoner complained of the admission as calculated to prejudice him before the jury.

One Eliza Anderson (a white woman), a witness for the State, was asked upon cross examination, if she was related to John Anderson (a man of color), and the object of this question was stated to be, her disparagement or discredit. Upon objection, the question was ruled out.

Verdict, Guilty; Rule for a New Trial discharged. Judgment, and Appeal.

Vance for the prisoner.
Attorney General, Boyden and *Clement, contra.*

Pearson, C. J. The case, as it now comes up, presents but few points, and no one of them calls for much discussion.

1st. On the argument, the point made upon the evidence offered to the court as preliminary to the admissibility of the acts and declarations of Ann Melton in evidence to the jury against the prisoner, was treated as if the question before this court was in regard to the *sufficiency* of the evidence to establish the fact of an agreement between Ann Melton and the prisoner to compass the death of Laura Foster; whereas, this court is confined to the question — was there *any evidence* tending to establish the fact? If so, his Honor's decision, as to its sufficiency, was upon *a question of fact*, which we cannot review. Looking at it in this point of view, it must be conceded that the point is against the prisoner.

2nd. "His honor erred in receiving as evidence to himself, the declaration of Ann Melton, to wit: the message and instructions given by her to the little girl sent by her to the prisoner." It does not appear on the record that this evidence was objected to as inadmissible. But, suppose it was objected to, we are of opinion that it was admissible on the ground that, although *naked* declarations of one are not admissible against the other, to show an agency or an agreement, yet this was not a naked declaration, like an admission or confession, but was a part of the act and, indeed, the most important part of it.

3rd. "The *words* used by Laura Foster ought not to have been received as evidence." We think that the evidence was admissible as a part of the act. It was so considered by us when the case was up before. *Vide ante*, 211.

4th. "The question put to the witness, Eliza Anderson, ought not to have been ruled out." There is not enough set out in the statement of the case to show the relevancy of this question, and we are confined to what appears in the statement of the case, treating it as a bill of exceptions on the part of the prisoner.

Neither of the two grounds, taken in support of the motion to arrest the judgment, are tenable. *State v. Lane*, 26 N. C., 113, is a conclusive answer to one, and the other is only objectionable as violating a rule of grammar. This does not vitiate a legal proceeding when the sense and meaning is clear. Indeed, as the plea of "not guilty" is several and not joint, it would seem to be most proper to use the verb in the singular number and to set out in the record that each person upon the arraignment *saith* "he is not guilty," "she is not guilty," instead of putting it in the form of a joint plea; but the authorities support the entry in either way.

There is no error. This opinion will be certified to the end, etc.

Per Curiam.   There is no error.

Cited: State v. McNoir, 93 N. C., 630; *State v. Arnold*, 107 N. C., 864.

NEWSPAPER ARTICLES
CONTEMPORARY WITH THE MURDER

The following article appeared in the New York *Herald* on May 2, 1868 and was reprinted in the Salisbury *Watchman and Old North State* on May 8.

THE DEATH PENALTY

Shocking Revelations of Crime and Depravity in North Carolina — Thos. Dula Hanged for the Murder of Laura Foster.

Statesville, N. C.
May 1, 1868

Today took place one of the most singular executions in the annals of crime and under the most extraordinary circumstances on record. A terrible crime was perpetrated and a trial that has not had its equal even in the Burdell trial followed. The evidence was entirely circumstantial; but at nearly half-past two, P. M., Thomas Dula suffered the death penalty, for the murder of Laura Foster, in the presence of nearly three thousand persons of his own race and color.

On the 28th day of May, 1866, a foul, inhuman murder was committed in the western portion of Wilkes County, in this State, the victim being Laura Foster, a beautiful, but frail girl, who was decoyed from her father's house in Caldwell County to a place in Wilkes known as the Bates Place, and here brutally murdered. The body was then removed about half a mile from the scene of the murder, and was placed in a grave already prepared for it. Late in August of the same year the body was found in a state of such decomposition that it was difficult to identify it. There was a deep gash in the left breast just above the heart; the wound had evidently been inflicted with a large knife or dagger, causing death instantaneously. It was also believed that the murdered woman was *encente* [pregnant].

The disappearance of Laura excited no alarm for several days, as it was supposed she had gone off to get married or to visit some acquaintances in Watauga county; but at length the opinion became general that she had been foully dealt with, and a general search was initiated, without success at the time. The community in the vicinity of this tragedy is divided into two entirely separate and distinct classes. The one occupying the fertile lands adjacent to the Yadkin river and its tributaries, is educated and intelligent, and the other, living on the spurs and ridges of the mountains, is ignorant, poor and depraved. A state of immorality unexampled in the history of any country exists among these people, and such a general system of freeloveism prevails that it is "a wise child that knows its father." This is the Bates place, where the body was discovered by blood marks, and where some ten or twelve families are living in the manner described. It is a poor country, covered with thickets and a dense undergrowth, and an attempt had been made to conceal the body by covering it with bushes.

Soon suspicion attached to Thos. Dula, a returned Confederate soldier, and one Pauline Foster, an illegitimate cousin of the deceased, and like her also frail, as the guilty parties. Pauline was then servant to Mrs. Melton, and between her and Dula a criminal intimacy was known to exist, and hence suspicion more particularly attached to the culprit, because Pauline had mysteriously disappeared for a time after the murder. Her character was the most abandoned of all, and under the influence of brandy she admitted when asked, that "Tom Dula and me killed Laura;" but apparently recollecting herself, would make no further revelations. A day subsequent to this, Pauline when [in] criminated by Mrs. Melton, confirmed the above statement, and she was arrested and confined in the jail of Wilkes county. Here she made a confession recriminating Mrs. Melton, who, she alleged, was jealous of Laura, and guided a party to the place where the body was discovered.

Meantime, Dula had fled the country, but was pursued and arrested in Tennessee, where he was found under an assumed name. He was then lodged in jail upon the evidence of Pauline, as was also Mrs. Melton, an accessory before the fact. True bills were found against both by the Grand Jury of Wilkes, but upon affidavit of the prisoners the trial was removed to Iredell county.

The most intense interest was maintained in the trial, which lasted several days, by the people here and of the surrounding counties. Nearly all the people on the Bates Place were examined, and the most extraordinary revelations of depraved morality were developed. Wilson Foster, the father of the deceased, testified that when he arose on the morning of Laura's disappearance, his horse was also gone; that he traced the animal to the Bates Place; that he knew the track by a peculiarity in one of the hoofs. He never saw his daughter alive again, but he saw and recognized her body; knew that Dula had been in the habit of visiting his daughter, and had seen them in bed together, and that they had two private conversations on the Monday and Wednesday respectively, preceding her disappearance. Further testimony went to show that Laura and Dula were both seen on the morning of the murder travelling by different routes from the direction of her home, to the Bates Place, with a view, as was supposed, to marry Dula; that Dula had borrowed a mattock, the implement with which the grave was dug, the day previous, and that he had been heard to say that he contracted a disease from the murdered girl for which he would be revenged upon her. It was also proven that Dula had changed his name, and when being brought back from Tennessee attempted to escape.

This comprised the essential testimony, and the witnesses generally appeared impressed with the idea that Dula was guilty, though some of them appeared anxious to affect an acquittal through fear of some of his reckless associates in the mountains. Another fact attempted to be proved was that the disease contracted by Dula from the murdered woman was imparted by him to Mrs. Melton, who forced him to the commission of the crime on that account. An appeal was granted from the first trial, and a second one had, when the same witnesses were examined, the same testimony elicited, and the same state of excitement existed. Gov. Vance and his assistant counsel for the defense, made powerful forensic efforts which were considered models of ability, but such was the evidence that no other verdict than that of guilty could be rendered.

Mrs. Ann Melton has not yet been tried, though she was present at both of Dula's trials, and, like him, heard his sentence without exhibiting any visible emotion. She is apparently about twenty-five years of age, is the illegitimate daughter of one Carlotta [Lotty] Foster, and is a most beautiful woman. She is entirely uneducated, and though living in the midst of depravity and ignorance has the manner

176

and bearing of an accomplished lady, and all the natural powers that should grace a high born beauty. This may in part account for the great influence she obtained over Dula, with whom she is illegitimately connected, and also for the fact that he persistently denies all knowledge of her participation in the murder.

Pauline Foster, the principal witness against both the accused, is remarkable for nothing but debasement, and may be dismissed with the statement that she has since married a white man and given birth to a Negro child.

Thomas Dula, the condemned man, is about twenty-five years old, five feet eleven inches high, dark eyes, dark curly hair, and though not handsome, might be called good-looking. He fought gallantly in the Confederate service, where he established a reputation for bravery; but since the war closed, has become reckless, demoralized and a desperado, of whom the people in his vicinity had a terror. There is everything in his expression to indicate the hardened assassin — a fierce glare of the eyes, a great deal of malignity, and a callousness that is revolting. He laughs and jokes when spoken to of his approaching end, and exhibits a shocking indifference as to the hereafter, refusing persistently all spiritual comfort from attending clergymen. Yesterday evening his sister and her husband who came with a wagon to take his body, sent him a note from his aged mother, entreating him to confess the truth for her sake, so that she would be satisfied of his guilt or innocence. But further than asking that they be allowed to see him, which request was refused, he said nothing. He still remained defiant, nor showed any signs of repentance, and seemed to have some hope of escape, though he did not say so. A confession had been looked for that might exonerate or implicate still further, his alleged accessory, Mrs. Melton, but this he refused to give, and left the impression that she is not guilty and shall not be "bowed" upon by him though the contrary is generally believed. He partook of a hearty supper, laughed and spoke lightly, but ere the jailor left him, it was discovered that his shackles were loose, a link in the chain being filed through with a piece of window glass, which was found concealed in his bed. While this was being adjusted, he glared savagely, and in a jocose manner said it had been so far a month past. Being at last left for the night by the jailor, he requested that Mr. Allison, one of his counsel, be sent for, and while charging him with the strictest injunctions to secrecy while he was living, handed him the following, written in a rude manner with a pencil: —

Statement of Thomas C. Dula — I declare that I am the only person that had any hand in the murder of Laura Foster.

April 30th, 1868

Besides this he had written a lengthy statement of his life, but without reference to the murder, which was intended as an exhortation to young men to live virtuously, and not to be led astray in paths of vice as he was. There was nothing remarkable in this document, though it covered fifteen pages.

Left alone in his cell on the last night of his earthly existence, the savage fortitude that had characterized his trials, sentence and imprisonment began to give way, and he nervously paced the floor as far as the chain would reach. This was only interrupted through the whole night by an attempt to court "Nature's sweet restorer," but in vain, if a fitful half hour is excepted, and the condemned, after the weary minutes of that night, saw the last sun he should ever behold shed its glorious light through the bars of the window. After breakfast he sent for his spiritual advisers, and seemed for the first time to make an attempt to pray; but still to them and all others denying his guilt or any knowledge of the murder. The theory seemed to be that he would show the people that he could die "game" with an awful crime resting upon his soul. Early in the morning he was baptized by the Methodist clergyman, and from that time engaged fervently in prayer; but when left alone was heard speaking incoherently, words occasionally dropping from his lips in relation to the murder, but nothing was intelligible. And thus wore away the last hours of the condemned.

So long had the execution been pending, and as the murder was committed in one county, and the trial had taken place in another, it became generally known throughout the entire western section of the State. By eleven o'clock, A. M., dense crowds of people thronged the streets, the great number of females being somewhat extraordinary. These, however, came mostly because it was a public day and afforded them an opportunity to make purchases, but a certain class indicated by a bronzed complexion, rustic attire, a quid of tobacco in their mouths, and a certain mountaineer look, were evidently attracted by the morbid curiosity to see an execution, so general among the ignorant classes of society. The preliminaries were all arranged by Sheriff Wasson. A gallows constructed of native pine, erected near the railroad depot in an old field — as there is no public place of execution in Statesville — was the place selected for the final tragedy. A guard had been summoned to keep back the crowd and enforce the terrible death penalty, and for the better preservation of order, the bar rooms were closed. The curious numbers of the people who had never seen a gallows before, visited the structure, eyeing it with strange feelings, and as it was merely two uprights, with a space of about ten feet and a cross piece on top, under which the cart with the condemned had to pass, many singular observations were made.

Previous to his being taken from the jail to the gallows, many of the condemned man's former companions in the army from the mountain region in which he lived appeared upon the streets, and some singular reminiscences of his former life were related. Among them, that it was generally believed he murdered the husband of a woman at Wilmington, in this State, during the war, with whom he had criminal intercourse. The opinion of all was that he was a terrible, desperate character, and from their knowledge of his former career an anxiety and singular curiosity was excited among them to see how he died. Few there were who pitied him dying, as they believed him guilty, without a confession, and none sympathized with him.

At eighteen minutes before one o'clock, the guard being formed in hollow square, the condemned was led forth attended by the Sheriff and some assistants, and with a smile upon his features, took his seat in the cart, in which was also his coffin, beside his brother in law. The procession moved slowly through the streets accompanied by large crowds, male and female, whites and blacks, many being in carriages and many on horseback and on foot. While on the way to the gallows he looked cheerful and spoke continually to his sister of the Scriptures, assuring her he had repented and that his peace was made with God. At the gallows throngs of people were already assembled, the number of females being almost equal to that of the males. The few trees in the field were crowded with men and boys, and under every imaginable shade that was present, were huddled together every imaginable species of humanity.

Soon the procession came in sight accompan (i) ed by horse-men dashing over the field dispersing the crowd, and at eight minutes past one the cart was halted under the gallows. The condemned man appeared unaffected by the sight, but talked incessantly to his sister and others of religion, trying if possible to assure them that he had repented. Upon being told by the Sheriff that he could address the assembled crowd, he arose and turning his dark eyes upon them spoke in a loud voice which rang back from the woods as if a demon there was mocking the tone and spirit of a wretch who well knew he was going into eternity with an unconfessed murder upon his mind and falsehood on his lips. He spoke of his early childhood, his parents, and his subsequent career in the army, referred to the dissolution of the Union, made blasphemous allusions to the Deity, invoking that name to prove assertions that he knew were some of them at least, false. The politics of the country he discussed freely, and upon being informed, in reply to a question of his, that Holden was elected Governor of North Carolina, he branded that person as a secessionist and a man that could not be trusted. His only reference to the murder was a half explanation of the country and the different roads and paths leading to the scene of the murder, in which his only anxiety was to show that some two or three of the witnesses swore falsely against him. He mentioned particularly one, James Isbell, who, he alleged, had perjured himself in the case, and concluded by saying that had there been no lies sworn against him he would not have been there. This concluded his speech, which had lasted nearly one hour, and after apparently affectionate farewell to his sister, who was then removed from the cart, the rope, which all the time had been around his neck, was thrown over the gallows and fastened. Standing there on the brink of eternity, this man, calm in the presence of the vast crowd, refused to admit publicly the murder of which they all believed him to be guilty.

At twenty-four minutes after two, P. M., the cart was moved, and the body of Thomas Dula was suspended between heaven and earth. The fall was about two feet, and the neck was not broken. He breathed about five minutes, and did not struggle, the pulse beating ten minutes, and in 13 minutes life was declared extinct by Dr. Campbell, attending surgeon. After hanging for twenty minutes the body was cut down and given over to the afflicted relatives of this terrible criminal.

Thus closed the career of a man, who, though young in years, ignorant and depraved in character, was one of the most confirmed and hardened criminals of the age in which he lived. As yet the written confession above given has not become known, and the greater anxiety is evinced among the people to ascertain whether he had left any confession that he might be too proud to make them in public. His reticence, however, is accounted for by the wish that he would not implicate his accomplice, Mrs. Ann Melton, now to be tried.

The following article on Tom Dula's first trial appeared in the Wilmington *Daily Dispatch* on October 26, 1866, copied from the Statesville *American*.

The trial of Thomas Dula for the Murder of Laura Foster — The first trial of Thos. Dula and Ann Melton for the murder of Laura Foster, which took place in Wilkes county some two or three months ago, and removed to Iredell, was commenced before Judge Buxton, last Friday morning. Upon application of Counsel, the case was separated, and Dula put first upon trial. The State's Attorney, W. F. Caldwell, Esq., was aided by Messrs. Clement and N. Boyden, and the prisoner defended by Messrs. R. M. Allison, R. F. Armfield and Gov. Vance. A very large number of witnesses were examined, and the case occupied the whole of Friday, Saturday and the following night; the judge gave his charge to the jury after midnight, and about daybreak the jury brought in a verdict against Thomas — *Guilty of Murder*. At 8 o'clock Sunday morning, the prisoner was sentenced to be hung on the 9th of November between the hours of 10 and 1 o'clock. And appeal was then taken to the Supreme Court.

All the evidence which led to the conviction was entirely circumstantial, but so connected by a concatenation of circumstances as to leave no reasonable doubt upon the minds of the Jury that the prisoner was at least one of the

182

parties that committed the murder. He was most ably defended by his counsel, as was likewise the prosecution. The patience of Judge Buxton during this long and tedious trial, and his humane and impartial charge to the Jury, in sifting the evidence and giving the prisoner the benefit of every reasonable doubt was but characteristic of an "upright Judge" and profound Jurist, who is an honor to the Bench and the State. During the trial the Court room was thronged with spectators and deep interest manifested in the result. A most foul murder of a young woman had been perpetrated — one who though frail, had been decoyed from her home by her betrayer under promises of marriage, and instead of a bridal chamber, received first a dagger in her heart and plunged uncoffined into a bloody grave. The calendar of crime contains not a darker deed.

The term of the Court having expired, the case of Ann Melton, the supposed confederate and accomplice of Dula, was continued, and, probably will be removed to another county.

The following brief statement of the complicity of parties in the tragedy as adduced by the testimony, may not be uninteresting to the public. Ann Melton is a married woman, young and beautiful, and a paramour of Dula's for several years, and had great influence over him. Laura Foster, a distant relative of Ann's, handsome and young, had likewise succumbed to his amours under promise of marriage, perhaps. Ann Melton and Dula's mother are near neighbors — a half mile apart. Laura Foster resided with her father, five miles distant. It was said that Ann became jealous of Laura and wanted her out of the way, and was perhaps present at the killing, if she did not aid in the deed. Thursday previous to the murder of Laura, which was on Friday, Dula borrowed a mattock of a neighbor, as he said, to work the road, but no doubt to dig a grave in the woods for Laura. That night, he is supposed to have visited Laura at her father's, and induced her to leave her home under some pretense, before day, she taking her father's horse and travelling one road, while he travelled a parallel road — both leading in the direction of his mother's house, and near Ann Melton's, where Laura's body was afterwards found buried, with a stab in the side. Both Dula and Laura were seen by neighbors as they passed along the two roads, on the morning of the fatal day, and Laura told her acquaintance who questioned her that she was going off to get married, etc. The horse which Laura rode afterwards returned to her father's. It was stated that Dula had threatened Laura from some cause which had arisen out of their intimacy.

The following article on the second trial of Tom Dula, January 1868, was carried in the Charlotte *Western Democrat*, February 4, 1868, copied from the Statesville *American*:

A Court of Oyer and Terminer, Judge Shipp presiding, was opened for the county of Iredell, at this place, Monday of last week. The case of Thomas Dula, charged with the murder of Laura Foster, was called on Tuesday. More than a hundred witnesses were summoned by the State, most of whom were present, and their examination occupied three days. The Solicitor, Mr. W. P. Caldwell, was aided by Messers. Boyden and Clement, and the accused was defended by Gov. Vance and Messrs. Furches and Allison. The pleadings began Friday afternoon and were concluded the following evening, when the Judge gave his charge to the Jury.

The murder was committed in the county of Wilkes, some eighteen months ago, where the parties resided, and the trial removed to Iredell; and, at the following term of our Superior Court, Dula was convicted and sentenced to be hanged. An appeal was taken to the Supreme Court and a new trial granted.

The Jury retired and in a short while returned with a verdict — "*Guilty*." Dula was sentenced to be hanged on the second Friday in February. An appeal was then applied for and granted to the Supreme Court now in session; with little hope, however, for a new trial. The prisoner was ably defended by his counsel. The address of Gov. Vance to the Jury was ingenious, eloquent, and distinguished for legal lore of the highest grade; but failed to inspire the minds of the Jury with a 'reasonable doubt.'

The Salisbury North State gives the following statement of the case:

"Thomas Dula, a young man of about twenty-five years of age, is charged with the murder of Miss Laura Foster. And Ann Melton is arraigned as accessory. It appears from the evidence that in May, 1866, Laura Foster arose from her bed in her father's house, about an hour before day, and taking her father's horse, which was tied that night near the door, travelled some few miles on a road to a place to which the horse was tracked, and near which her body was subsequently found in the woods. Dula and Mrs. Melton were absent from their homes the night on which Laura Foster left her father's and were seen next morning in the neighborhood of the place where the body of Laura Foster was found buried. It is charged that Mrs. Melton was jealous of the attention paid Laura Foster by Dula, and therefore aided and abetted in the murder. The incidents, as developed before the jury, were of the most thrilling character."

WHAT REALLY HAPPENED?

As nearly as can be determined from the records, the following account summarizes the Tom Dula-Laura Foster tragedy:

Around March 1, 1866, Pauline Foster left Watauga County and travelled to the Reedy Branch community of Wilkes, supposedly to visit her grandfather. Her real motive was to secure treatment from Dr. George N. Carter for syphilis, which she had contracted back in her home county. Her plan succeeded. She encountered James and Ann Melton, who offered her 21 dollars to work for them in the fields and about the house for the duration of the summer. She accepted the job, planning to use the money to pay for treatment of her disease and the medicines required.

Sometime after the middle of March, Tom Dula began to visit Laura Foster regularly, at least once a week. Frequently he would spend the night at the Foster house, sometimes sleeping with Laura. At the same time, he was carrying on intercourse with his neighbors, Mrs. Ann Melton, Pauline Foster, who lived with the Meltons, and probably Caroline

Barnes. Soon after the beginning of his relationship with Laura Foster, around the last of March or the first of April, he visited Dr. George N. Carter with syphilis in its primary state (the appearance of a hard chancre) and asked for treatment. He told Dr. Carter that he had contracted the disease from Laura Foster.

On Sunday, May 13, Tom Dula stopped off at the home of R. D. Hall, on his way from church, and told Hall he was diseased and he intended to "put through" the one who had diseased him. Hall said to him, "Tom, I wouldn't do that."

On Sunday, May 20, Tom Dula visited Laura Foster for about an hour, talking with her. The following Wednesday, May 23, he returned to the Foster home, visiting Laura again. Wilson Foster, Laura's father, was away when Tom arrived but returned around noon, to find Tom and Laura sitting close together by the fire talking (cooking was done on the open fireplace). Tom left before the noon meal. On his way back down the river, he was seen by Betsy Scott three miles from the Foster home, walking.

Thursday morning, May 14, Ann Melton told Pauline that Tom had given her the pock (syphilis) and that he had contracted it from Laura Foster. She said that James Melton, her husband, also had it and she would fool him and have her revenge too. She said that she intended to "have do" with Melton and make him think he had given her the disease. She also said she was going to kill Laura Foster and if Pauline Foster, to whom she was talking, left home that day or talked about what she had said with anybody, she (Ann) would kill her.

After this talk, Ann left the house. A little later Tom Dula came to James Melton's home from the direction of the "Ridge Road," the way Ann had gone. He told Pauline he wanted some alum for sores in his mouth. He said he had met Ann up on the ridge, and she had told him to get the alum at the house. He also asked to borrow a canteen. Pauline gave him the canteen and he left.

Later that morning, Tom Dula visited Lotty Foster, Ann's mother, and borrowed a mattock. Thomas Foster, Lotty's son, was home and heard Tom Dula say he "wanted to work some devilment out of himself." Tom took the mattock and started off down Reedy Branch in the direction of his mother's house, where he lived. Shortly thereafter, Martha Gilbert saw Tom digging with the mattock along the path near the branch and about a hundred yards from his mother's house. It turned out to be only about two hundred to three hundred yards from where he was digging to the spot where the grave was later discovered. Martha Gilbert asked him what he was doing, and he said he was making the road wider so he could walk it at night.

Carson Dula came to James Melton's house around 10:00 a. m. Thursday and brought the canteen Tom had borrowed, filled with liquor. When Pauline Foster returned from the field at noon, the liquor was there. After the noon meal, Ann took a drink of the liquor and said it (the canteen of liquor) was for Tom Dula. Then she left, carrying the canteen. Ann went directly to her mother's house with it. Tom Dula returned to Lotty Foster's a little later in the afternoon without the mattock, and he and Ann Melton left there together around 3:00 p. m. Ann was gone from her home for the rest of that day and the following night. Washington Anderson visited James Melton's cabin for about two hours that night; he found James Melton, Jonathan Gilbert, and Pauline Foster there, but Ann Melton was missing.

Ann Melton returned home an hour before daybreak on Friday, May 25, undressed, and got into bed with Pauline Foster. She told Pauline that she, her mother, and Tom Dula "had laid out all night and drunk the canteen of liquor." When Pauline got up to prepare breakfast, she found that Ann's dress and shoes were wet. While Pauline and James Melton were eating breakfast, Washington Anderson came in and stayed a few minutes. He noticed that Ann's shoes were wet but did not see her dress.

Ann was still in bed when Pauline started to the field to help plant corn. Before she had gone far, she noticed that the cows had come (cattle ranged without pastures and the crops were fenced in) and returned to the house for a pail in which to milk. When she entered the house, Tom Dula was there bent over Ann Melton's bed, in low conversation with her. Tom asked Pauline what she intended to do that day, and when she told him she would "drop corn," he said that it was too hot to work.

Thursday evening, May 24, Wilson Foster went to bed, leaving Laura up. An hour before daybreak on Friday, Laura got up and went outside for a short while. (The sun rises at 6:35 EST on May 25. Daybreak arrives around 6:00 or a little before.) Laura obviously had a conference with Tom Dula. She came back inside, went to the closet, took out some of her clothing, and made a bundle of them. Soon afterwards she went back outside, untied her father's mare, and mounted her. She headed down the river road toward Elkville, holding the bundle of clothing in her lap.

About a mile from home, Laura encountered Betsy Scott near A. Scott's house. Betsy Scott had talked with Laura two or three days earlier about her (Laura) and Tom Dula, and Laura had confided in her. Apparently, she had told Betsy that Tom intended to marry her. Betsy Scott asked her that Friday morning if Tom had come to see her that morning, and Laura answered that Tom had come just before day. Betsy Scott then asked Laura where Tom was, and Laura explained that he had gone around "to flank Manda Barnes' house." Betsy said if she were in Laura's place she would have been farther along the road by that time of day. Laura said she had started as soon as she could. When Betsy Scott asked her where she planned to meet Tom, Laura told her she would meet him at the Bates place. Laura left her then and continued on down the road in the direction of Elk Creek and the Bates place beyond.

That same Friday morning, May 25, after Tom Dula left

Laura Foster, he headed eastward along a foot path which paralleled the river road and lay north of it. The distance from Wilson Foster's house to the Bates place by way of the river road and the Stony Fork road was six miles, by the path Tom Dula took, only five miles. A little after sunup (around 6:45), Tom passed through Carl Carlton's yard, heading east. He stopped and talked with Carlton for a few minutes. He asked Carlton if the path led to Kendall's house, then continued on his way.

Before he reached the Kendall home, a mile or so east of Carlton's, he met Hezekiah Kendall, around 8:00 a. m. Kendall asked Tom if he had been "after the woman." Tom said, "No, I have quit that." Tom's trousers were wet with dew, Kendall noted. Mrs. James Scott, who lived on the same path east of Kendall's, was the next person to see Tom Dula that morning. He reached her home just after breakfast, and she invited him in to eat. He sat on her steps a short while and rested but did not eat. After a few minutes, he got up and left, arriving at James Melton's house just before Pauline returned for the milk pail.

After his conference with Ann and his encounter with Pauline Foster, Tom turned south toward the Stony Fork road, but stopped at Lotty Foster's house on the hill above. He asked Lotty for some milk, and she gave him a half gallon. He took it and headed down the path toward the Stony Fork road. Thomas Foster saw him a little later on that road, just before the turnoff to the Bates place.

Mary Dula, Tom's mother, left home early Friday morning, after discovering that Tom was missing from the house. When she returned at noon, he was lying in bed. He ate and stayed about the house until around sundown. Around 3:00 p. m. Mary Dula left for a short while to look for her cows and encountered Carson and Jesse Gilbert on the path between her house and the Stony Fork road. While she was preparing supper, Tom "went out about the barn," she thought, where he remained for a while; but about this time of the same day, Lotty and Thomas Foster saw Tom Dula heading in the direction of the Bates place.

Tom Dula returned home, ate his supper, then left again just after dark and was gone for an hour, according to his mother. Returning home, he undressed and went to bed, complaining of chills. His mother said that she heard him moaning during the night and bent over him once to kiss him. If he got up during the night and left, she did not hear him. He was in bed the next morning and did not leave until after breakfast. (It is reasonable to believe that Tom was gone much longer than an hour just before dark that Friday, returning to the Bates place, and that he left again during the night, to join Ann Melton, who had slipped away from her own home.)

Wilson Foster got up "around daybreak" (6:00 a. m.) Friday, May 25, and found Laura and his mare missing. He set out in search of them. One of the mare's tracks was "peculiar" because he had started to trim the hoof but had left it unfinished and with a sharp point to it. It was easy to follow, and he tracked the mare past A. Scott's house, all the way down the river road to the Stony Fork road, and along it as far as the Bates place. There he lost it in an old field. He gave up the search and went to James Scott's house, where he ate breakfast and told of his search. From there, he went to James Melton's, arriving just after Tom had gone. Ann was there in bed. He stayed about fifteen minutes, then left and visited several other houses, inquiring about Laura and his mare.

Wilson Foster returned to James Melton's house around nightfall and stayed there for two or three hours. Pauline Foster, Thomas Foster, Will Holder, Washington Anderson, Jonathan Gilbert, and James and Ann Melton were there. Everyone was joking and having a good time. Thomas Foster burned Wilson's beard as a practical joke. It was at this gathering that Wilson Foster made the statements about not caring what happened to Laura just so long as he got his mare back (according to Pauline Foster's testimony) and that he would kill Laura if he found her. It was also on this occasion that Pauline was said to have offered to get the mare back for a quart of liquor and to have made the remark about Laura running off with a colored man.

Wilson Foster left James Melton's house later in the evening and spent the night with Francis Melton. When he reached home the next day, Saturday, May 26, he found his mare there. The lead rope had been broken, about two feet of it left dangling from the halter.

Any detailed discussion of what happened at the Bates place can be, at best, only conjecture. It was the State's hypothesis that the grave was dug on Thursday or Thursday night and that Laura Foster was killed on Friday or Friday night, the implication being that she was buried soon thereafter. This theory was proved to the satisfaction of two juries.

Tom Dula borrowed the mattock from Lotty Foster on Thursday morning, and Martha Gilbert saw him digging, a short time later, within two to three hundred yards of where the grave was later found. It would have been an easy matter for Tom to conceal the mattock in the bushes near the grave site. He returned to Lotty Foster's later in the afternoon without the mattock, and he and Ann Melton left together with the canteen of liquor around 3:00 p. m. He and Ann were missing from their homes for the remainder of the afternoon and night. That was the logical time to dig the grave. On May 24 they would have had plenty of daylight during which to dig a grave between 3:30 and nightfall, especially one only two and a half feet deep, narrow, and too short for a woman of average size.

On Friday morning, May 25, Tom Dula arrived at the Bates place carrying the half gallon of milk soon after Laura Foster. (Although Tom had a mile less to cover than Laura and left her house ahead of her, she rode horseback and Tom stopped several times to talk and rest along the path he travelled.) If Tom had killed Laura soon after they met, Ann Melton could not have assisted him because at that time she was home in bed. Of course there is no reason to believe he did not commit the crime alone. Furthermore, if Laura had died that early in the morning, rigor mortis would have prevented the bending of her legs so that she could be placed in the grave the following night. It is logical to speculate that Tom Dula had planted the canteen of liquor at the Bates place the day before, and that he drank with Laura until she was intoxicated and was then able to talk her into waiting for him at the Bates place all day Friday. If he had been able to convince her to take her father's mare and meet him there, it should not have been as difficult to talk her into waiting for him.

Tom returned to the Bates place just after nightfall that Friday. Again he was alone; Ann Melton was at home with her husband, Pauline Foster, and several other visitors. This was the logical time for the murder. Laura Foster would have grown impatient from her long wait. If the murder was committed at this time, Tom had to do it alone, without the aid of Ann Melton. Pauline Foster testified that he habitually carried a Bowie knife in a pocket in his coat, and the description of the murder weapon in the indictment resembles such a weapon except for the length. A discolored spot with an offensive odor near one of the trees to which the mare had been tied convinced the two juries that Laura had been killed at the Bates place and her body carried to the waiting grave.

It is reasonable to speculate as follows: Tom Dula returned home and went to bed after this visit to the Bates place (the one just after nightfall on May 25). During the night, he arose and left the house again, without his mother's knowledge. He met Ann Melton somewhere along the Stony Fork road, and they returned to the Bates place. They carried Laura's body down along the ridge throuugh the forest to the grave, prepared on Thursday night, a half to three-quarters of a mile from where she was killed, according to Col. Isbell's map. Wade Gilbert said that Tom Dula and Ann Melton carried the corpse in a sheet tied to a pole, which they held between them. In any case, Laura would not have been too much of a burden for the two of them; the *Herald* article described her as frail. They buried her in darkness and returned to their respective beds, where Tom Dula's mother found him the next day and where Pauline Foster testified that Ann was also.

Whether one believes the murder and burial occurred in precisely this manner is not important. The fact is that Laura was murdered either early Friday morning just after arriving at the Bates place, by Dula alone, Friday afternoon by Dula alone, Friday evening while his mother was preparing supper, by Dula alone, or sometime Friday night or early Saturday morning, by Tom Dula and Ann Melton together.

About the same time Wilson Foster was discovering his mare at his cabin early Saturday morning, May 26, Tom Dula arrived at James Melton's home. He and Ann conversed for a half hour in low voices. Tom told Pauline Foster he had come for his fiddle and to get his shoes mended. Pauline Foster remarked to him, "I thought you had run away with Laura Foster."

He laughed and replied, "I have no use for Laura Foster."

Tom Dula left for home but returned that night with his fiddle and played until bedtime. He spent the night, sleeping with James Melton.

Early that same Saturday morning, Ann Melton told Pauline Foster that she had gotten up during the night, and she (Pauline) and Thomas Foster had not missed her. She also said "she'd done what she had said." She had killed Laura Foster.

Some of the events which occurred that summer between the murder and the discovery of the body, around September 1, can be dated and some of them cannot, but the important ones can at least be placed in chronological order. Soon after the Saturday Wilson Foster's mare returned home, parties began to search in the vicinity of the Bates place for Laura Foster's corpse. Men came from several miles away to help. My grandfather John Witherspoon West, who lived on Lewis Fork Creek, was one of them. J. W. Winkler searched for seven or eight days. At first no clues could be found indicating Laura's fate. Events reached a minor climax four weeks after Laura disappeared.

Sunday, June 24, J. W. Winkler and his neighbors were out searching and formed a line "like a line of battle." They searched the forest from near Tom Dula's home to the Bates place. This time they found a piece of rope tied to a dogwood tree near the latter spot. The rope was of flax and the broken end matched the end of the rope which was fastened to the halter on Wilson Foster's mare. A hundred yards from the dogwood (Col. Isbell said 200 yards) were signs that the mare had also been tied to a whiteoak, including two piles of dung. Some fifteen or twenty feet off from this tree, the searchers found a discolored spot about the size of a man's hand with an offensive odor. They decided the spot was blood, Laura Foster's blood.

Around Friday or Saturday, June 22 or 23, James Melton told Tom Dula in the presence of Pauline Foster that "it was reported about [by the] Hendrickses that Dula had killed Laura Foster." Tom Dula laughed and said, "They will have to prove it and perhaps take a beating besides." On Sunday, June 24, the same day the search party found the rope and blood spot, James Melton warned Tom Dula in the presence of Pauline that he (Tom) was about to be arrested for Laura Foster's murder. Tom cursed the Hendrickses as a result of this information. (Members of the Hendricks family who appeared as witnesses at the trial were M. C., Gay, Leoander, and Micajah — spelling taken from transcript.)

The next day, Monday, June 25, Tom Dula returned to James Melton's and went from there to visit the Hendricks family. During the afternoon Ann Melton tore a clapboard from the log wall of the Melton cabin at the head of her bed, made a hole through the mud chinking between the logs, and ran a string through the hole. She drove a nail into a log outside the cabin, tying one end of the string to the nail and placing the other end in her bed. She also placed a knife under the head of the bed. Apparently she intended to tie the end of the string in her bed to her wrist so that she could be awakened quietly from outside the house.

Tom returned from the Hendricks home to James Melton's just after nightfall. James Melton had gone to bed, but Ann and Pauline Foster were still up. Tom was depressed and did not say much. Pauline offered to prepare a bed for him, but Tom declined, saying that he intended to go home. However, he changed his mind and threw himself down on one of the beds with his clothes on and began to cry. Ann Melton lay down on Pauline's bed, and Pauline got in behind her. She discovered that Ann Melton was weeping too. Ann Melton arose and went outside and Tom followed her. Soon thereafter he returned to the room and raised the head of the bed (apparently to get the knife). Pauline asked him what was wrong, and he told her to come outside and he would tell her.

Pauline followed Tom outside, and he told her "they" were telling lies on him (telling he killed Laura Foster, which he denied to Pauline) and he was going to leave (the county). He said that he would return Christmas for his mother and would take Ann with him also. Tom and Ann embraced, weeping, and Tom told her good-by and left. When Ann and Pauline re-entered the cabin, James Melton asked Ann why she was crying, and she told him that Tom Dula was leaving.

Tom left that Monday night, June 25 (or early Tuesday morning), walking toward Watauga County. His logical route would have been up the Elk Creek road, through the community of Triplett, and on up to the Boone Trail, which ran along the Blue Ridge. He would have continued west to present-day Perkinsville, just east of Boone, then turned almost due north along one of the wilderness trails through Sands to Meat Camp Creek. Here, he probably turned north-west, following the creek for some distance, then crossing through Rich Mountain Gap between Rich and Snake mountains, descending to the community of Zionville beyond. From Zionville, it was only two or three miles across the state line to Trade, Tennessee, where James W. M. Grayson's farm was located.

On Thursday of that week the sheriff of Wilkes County received the following warrant:

To the Sheriff of Wilkes County

Greetings

Whereas information upon oath hath been made upon the oath of Wilson Foster of Caldwell County that his daughter Laura Foster late of said county mysteriously disappeared from her home, under circumstances as to induce him to believe as that she had been murdered or otherwise foully dealt with by certain persons under suspicion (to wit, Thomas Dula, Ann Pauline Melton, Ann Pauline Dula, and Granville Dula of the County of Wilkes). This is therefore to command you to arrest the bodies of the said Thomas Dula, Ann Pauline Melton, Ann Pauline Dula and Granville Dula of the county of Wilkes if to be found and have them before me or some other justice of the peace to answer the above charge and be further dealth with according to law. Herein fail not. Given under my hand and seal this 28th day of June, 1866.

Pickins Carter JP

It is difficult to be certain, but there is good reason to believe that Pickins Carter was a justice of the peace in the Elkville township and that he held his "court" at Cowels

Store there. According to the testimony of one of the witnesses at the trials, a hearing was held at Cowels Store. This trial or hearing by Carter was held on Friday, June 29, and Justice Carter found the defendants "Ann Melton, Ann Dula, and Granville Dula not guilty of the charges alleged against them." Thomas Dula's name was not mentioned, and, in fact, he was at this time a fugitive from arrest as a result of the above justice of the peace warrant. Ann Dula and Granville Dula are never mentioned elsewhere in papers related to the trials, not even as witnesses, and it is impossible to identify them.

Giving Tom Dula a week to cover the serpentine roads between Reedy Branch and Trade, Tennessee, with a brief layover in Watauga County, where he changed his name to Hall, he would have arrived at Col. James Grayson's farm around Monday, July 2. He worked there for about a week, until around July 10, when he fled westward toward Johnson City to escape Jack Adkins and Ben Ferguson, who were deputized to bring him back to Wilkesboro. Col. Grayson, aided by the two deputies, captured him late the same day, and he was delivered to the Wilkesboro jail the next day, around July 11, a Wednesday.

Three weeks after Tom Dula left the community of Reedy Branch, Pauline Foster and her brother also left and returned to their home in Watauga. That would have been around July 14. By that time Tom Dula was already in the Wilkesboro jail, according to Pauline's testimony in the unidentified transcript. During the time she was in Watauga County, Pauline apparently took a trip into Tennessee for some reason never disclosed. Shortly after she returned to Watauga from Tennessee, Ann Melton and Sam Foster came after her. (Sam Foster is never identified but was probably Ann Melton and Thomas Foster's brother.) Ann told Pauline that "they" were talking about arresting her (Pauline) and induced her to return to Reedy Branch with her and Sam.

About three weeks after Pauline Foster returned from

Watauga, in early August, probably, Ann Melton approached her, weeping, and said, "Poor Tom. I wonder if he will be hung. Are you his friend? I am. Are you a friend of mine? I want to show you Laura Foster's grave. They have pretty well quit looking for it. I want to see whether it looks suspicious." If it did look suspicious, Ann at first talked of digging up the body and burying it in a cabbage patch. Then she changed her mind and considered cutting it up and disposing of the pieces. (This testimony might be the origin of the folk myth that Laura was mutilated so that her body would fit into the short grave.)

Pauline Foster went with Ann to find the grave. They went from the Melton house, past Lotty Foster's cabin, crossed Reedy Branch in the valley below, and climbed a ridge. They came to a pine log where the dirt appeared to have been rooted up by hogs. Ann said the grave was farther up the ridge, between trees and ivy bushes. She covered up the disturbed earth about the log with leaves. Pauline refused to go any farther. Ann wanted her to continue with her to the grave and cursed her all the way back down the ridge to the branch.

About a week after this, Jack Adkins and Ben Ferguson visited the Melton house. They were all sitting around talking, and Ben Ferguson remarked that he believed Pauline had helped kill Laura Foster and had run off to Tennessee (or Watauga — Pauline gave two versions of the remark).

Pauline said, "Yes, I and Dula killed her, and I ran away to Tennessee."

Within a few days of this conversation, Pauline and Ann had the fight at the home of Mrs. James Scott over Pauline's remark to Ferguson. "Two or three weeks" after the remark, Pauline was arrested and placed in the Wilkesboro jail as a suspected accessory in the murder. That was very likely around August 28, or during the week of that date.

Pauline was questioned while in jail and told everything she knew. As a result of her description of the trip to the pine log with Ann Melton, Pauline was taken out of jail (around September 1) and returned to Reedy Branch to guide a search party to the area of the grave. Apparently, there were several people in the group, and they split up, going in different directions from the log Pauline had shown them. Col. James Isbell and David Horton, the latter on horseback, were paired together, and they found the grave, after about an hour's search, within seventy-five yards of the log.

When the corpse was uncovered, Dr. George N. Carter was summoned to examine it. The flesh was off the face. Laura Foster wore a checkered cotton dress and a dark cloak. The bundle of clothes had been placed over her face. The body was lying on its right side, with the face turned up. The grave was two and a half feet deep, very narrow, and not long enough for the body. The legs were drawn up (not broken) so the corpse would fit into the grave. Laura Foster had been stabbed on the left breast, between the third and fourth ribs. There were marks in the grave such as a mattock would have made.

Laura Foster's corpse was carried down out of the forest, placed in a casket, and buried at German's Hill, where the grave can be seen today. Ann Melton was arrested as a consequence of Pauline Foster's testimony at the hearing following the discovery of the body, and Pauline was released. It is interesting to note that Tom Dula was held in jail at Wilkesboro from approximately July 10 until Laura Foster's corpse was found, about September 1, on a justice of the peace warrant without bail and without a corpse to prove a murder had, in fact, been committed.

In brief conclusion, a grand jury found a true bill against Tom Dula and Ann Melton at the opening of the fall term of Superior Court in Wilkesboro, October 1, 1866, Judge Ralph P. Buxton presiding. Ex-Governor Zebulon B. Vance, then in private practice in Charlotte, for some reason agreed to defend the prisoners without compensation, assisted by

Richard M. Allison and Robert F. Armfield. W. P. Caldwell, solicitor for the district, prosecuted, aided by Nathaniel Boyden and John M. Clement. Vance asked for a severance (Dula and Ann Melton to be tried separately), which was granted, and a change of venue. The trial was moved to Statesville, in Iredell County, and tried there during fall term of the same court session, Judge Buxton, presiding.

The trial ran all day Friday, October 19, 1866, all day Saturday, and Saturday evening. Judge Buxton gave his charge to the jury after midnight, and the jury apparently deliberated all night, bringing in a verdict of *guilty of murder* around daybreak. At 8:00 a. m. Sunday, October 21, Tom Dula was sentenced to be hanged on November 9, between ten o'clock in the morning and one o'clock in the afternoon, but an appeal was taken to the state Supreme Court.

The Supreme Court took the case and found sufficient cause for a new trial. Tom Dula's case appeared on the docket of the spring term, 1867, Superior Court in Iredell County, but the prisoner requested a continuance because three of his witnesses failed to appear, and the request was granted. The case appeared on the docket of the next session of Superior Court, fall term, 1867. This time the State asked for a continuance because three of the State's witnesses failed to appear. This request was granted also.

To end the delay, a special court of Oyer and Terminer was convened in Statesville on Monday, January 20, 1868, Judge William Shipp presiding. The prosecutor and assistants remained the same as in the first trial. In this trial, David M. Furches replaced Allison; otherwise the Defense remained unchanged. Again the jury found Tom Dula guilty of murder. Judge Shipp sentenced him to be hanged on February 14, 1868, between 10:00 a. m. and 4:00 p. m.

A second appeal was taken to the Supreme Court. This time no error was found and the sentence stood. At the spring term of Superior Court in Iredell, April 17, 1868, Judge Anderson Mitchell set a new date for the execution.

Tom Dula was hanged on May 1, 1868, near the old depot in Statesville, a cart used for a scaffold and a crude construction of uprights with a crossbeam as the gallows. His body was returned to Elkville by his sister and her husband and buried. Ann Melton was tried during the fall term of Superior Court, 1868, in Wilkesboro and exonerated.

A monument, mutilated by vandals and containing the incorrect execution date, now marks the traditional grave site, beside the old Lenoir-Wilkesboro road south of the Yadkin River, on land which in recent years was a part of the Sam Jones estate. But it would not be surprising to learn some day that this tradition is also a myth and that Tom Dula's body was buried in the hills on Reedy Branch, closer to his mother's cabin.

A MODERN LAWYER'S VIEW
OF THE TOM DULA CASE
by
Ted G. West, Attorney at Law, Lenoir, N. C.

I have been familiar with the legend and folklore of the Tom Dula case since early childhood, having heard my parents and other persons living in the general area where the crime was committed discuss it on many occasions. I, of course, have heard many of them express the opinion that Tom Dula was not guilty of the offense for which he was hanged. However, after reaching adulthood and studying law and having been engaged in the practice of law for a number of years, I have tended to put little credence in such stories because of an awareness that the gossip concerning most highly publicized or controversial cases have little relation to the actual evidence presented at the trial of the cause. In criminal cases as in many other aspects of life, people tend to believe what they want to believe, not what the evidence shows. Therefore, upon being asked to review the material in this volume and to make some comments upon the legal aspects of the case as a lawyer, I approached it with the full expectation of concluding that Tom Dula was given a fair trial with due process of law, found guilty by a jury of his peers beyond a reasonable doubt, and paid the supreme penalty which the law provides. I was somewhat surprised after reviewing this volume to come to the conclusion that at least according to the legal standards of today, Tom Dula's conviction and ultimate execution leaves a great deal of room for doubt.

There are at least four aspects of the Tom Dula case which I think bear interesting comment from the standpoint of a lawyer. I would like to discuss briefly each of the four in order.

Tom Dula was first charged with the crime by warrant dated June 28, 1866, after he had removed himself from Wilkes County to the State of Tennessee. His arrest in Tennessee and removal to Wilkes County was, to say the least, most informal, compared to the legal standards required to extradite a person from another state's jurisdiction under today's procedures. At the time of the issuance of the warrant and at the time that Tom Dula was removed from Tennessee to Wilkes County, Laura Foster's body had not yet been discovered and there was, therefore, only a mere suspicion current in the neighborhood that a crime had actually been committed. As far as the authorities knew, Laura Foster could have been in Tennessee with Tom Dula or could have been in any other place that she might have decided to go. In spite of this fact, Tom was charged with the crime of murder, removed from Tennessee and placed in jail in Wilkes County. He stayed in jail from the time of his arrival in Wilkes County until Laura Foster's body was discovered in late August or early September, 1866, a period of approximately two months. During this time there was apparently no effort to give him a hearing, to set a bond, or to afford him any of the other constitutional and procedural safeguards current in today's legal procedures.

There can be little doubt that if the same event occurred today in a like manner, and if Tom Dula had not agreed to return to Wilkes County voluntarily, the Governor of Tennessee would certainly not have extradited him against his will until the body was discovered and proof that a crime had been committed had been presented to the authorities. In addition to this factor, once he was removed to Wilkes County, he would certainly have been entitled to an arraignment within a reasonable period of time and upon the failure of the State to prove at the arraignment that a crime had been committed, he would have been set free until such time as the body of Laura Foster was discovered. I can, therefore, only conclude that his incarceration in the Wilkes County jail for a period of almost sixty days was unlawful and was certainly a violation of his constitutional rights. This fact, however, has little to do with the ultimate issue of his guilt or innocence. It could have been an important aspect of the case only if during the period of the unlawful confinement, Tom Dula had confessed to the crime or if any of the evidence presented at the trial of the cause had been obtained as a direct result of his unlawful confinement. In either of these events, the confession and evidence would not have been admitted into the trial. However, since neither of these events occurred, the question of his proper extradition from Tennessee and the question of his unlawful confinement prior to the discovery of the body is only of passing interest, and as stated before, has little to do with the ultimate issue of his guilt or innocence of the crime for which he was executed.

The other two factors in his case which should be commented upon do bear upon the question of his guilt or innocence.

It is an elementary rule of procedural law that statements made by another person not made in the presence of the defendant on trial are not admissible into evidence. This rule has as its basis the reasoning that, first, the statements of the party not in the presence of the defendant cannot be denied by the defendant at the time the statement is made, and second, the statement is not subject to the cross-examination of the defendant or his lawyer. There is one exception to this general rule of evidentiary law which is pertinent to the Tom Dula case — that is, that if prior to the commission of the crime there is a conspiracy or common design to commit an unlawful act between the defendant and the person making the statement, then the statements by the co-conspirator not made in the presence of the defendant may be admitted into evidence at the defendant's trial. This is based on the premise that the pre-existence of the conspiracy makes the statement of one the statement of the other. As the records show, at the trial of Tom Dula, certain statements of Ann Melton made after the date of the death of Laura Foster were admitted into evidence against Tom Dula based upon a finding of the trial judge that there had been a common design or conspiracy to murder between Tom Dula and Ann Melton. A review of the evidence presented in this volume shows clearly, I think, that this ruling by the trial judge was erroneous.

Ann Melton and Tom Dula, the evidence shows, had been engaged in an illicit romance for some years prior to the death of Laura Foster. Tom Dula visited Ann Melton regularly, almost nightly, and in fact slept in the same bed with her with Ann Melton's husband present in the same room. His association with her was obvious and common knowledge throughout the community. The only evidence of any conspiracy between her and Tom Dula to commit murder was certain testimony by witnesses that some time prior to the disappearance of Laura Foster, Ann Melton and Tom Dula had been seen together, had carried on whispered conversations, and had generally acted in a somewhat suspicious manner. In view of their prior relationship, these meetings, conferences and consultations are certainly subject to some interpretation other than that they were conspiring to commit a crime since there was not the slightest evidence of any direct conversation between the two concerning the commission of the crime. One can only conclude therefore, in retrospect, that for the trial judge to hold as a matter of law that there was a conspiracy between Ann Melton and Tom Dula pre-existing the disappearance of Laura Foster to murder her is certainly a loose and prejudicial interpretation of their acts and conduct at that time. If this be true, then any of the statements made by Ann Melton not in the presence of Tom Dula which were admitted at the trial of the cause against Tom Dula should have been excluded.

The fourth and most important aspect of the review of the record which should be commented upon has to do with the evidence proper admitted against the defendant upon which the jury based their verdict. In order to view this in its proper light, it is necessary at this time to give a short resume of the substantive evidence upon which the jury based their finding.

An analysis of the testimony of all the witnesses put on the witness stand by the State shows the following: That Tom Dula had syphilis and on one occasion stated he was going to do harm to the person who gave it to him and on another occasion stated that Laura Foster was the person who gave him the disease. That on the day before Laura Foster's disappearance, Tom Dula was seen with a mattock in his hand near the spot where her grave was discovered some three months later. That the night before Laura's disappearance both Tom Dula and Ann Melton were absent from their homes, and that early on the morning of her disappearance, Laura Foster was seen riding her father's horse with a bundle of clothing in the direction of Bates' Place and that on the same morning Tom Dula was seen going in the same direction. It was further put into evidence that the horse which Laura Foster was riding came home with a part of her halter missing and the missing part of the halter was later discovered near where she and Tom Dula had been seen. That afterwards something that looked like blood was seen near that spot and that some time after Laura Foster disappeared, Dula fled the country. It was further testified to that the grave was ultimately discovered because of certain disclosures that had been made by Ann Melton and that the grave was within a fairly short distance of Tom Dula's house and was within 100 or 200 yards of the spot where Tom Dula had been seen with the mattock the day before Laura Foster disappeared.

This is the sum total of the evidence presented to the jury, from which it concluded beyond a reasonable doubt that Tom Dula killed Laura Foster. It is obvious that all of this evidence is completely circumstantial. It is further obvious that it certainly raises the suspicion that Tom Dula murdered Laura Foster. That the evidence raises such a suspicion is not the purpose of this analysis. Its purpose is to determine whether or not Tom Dula would have been convicted and executed for the crime under the evidence as presented according to today's legal procedures and legal standards of guilt.

It is a settled rule of law in North Carolina that circumstantial evidence alone is sufficient to support a conviction for a crime. This is true, provided, however, that the circumstantial evidence is so strong and positive that: First, the circumstances pointing to guilt of the defendant must exclude every other reasonable hypothesis and point unerringly toward the guilt of the defendant being tried; and second, it convinces a jury of a prisoner's guilt beyond a reasonable doubt.

I do not think it takes a lawyer to conclude, after reviewing this record, that the evidence presented against Tom Dula does not meet at least one of these standards. The evidence obviously convinced the jury beyond a reasonable doubt of his guilt or it would not have found him guilty. The evidence is not, however, subject only to the interpretation of the guilt of Tom Dula and therefore does not exclude every reasonable hypothesis. It shows only a motive and the opportunity which is generally held insufficient to support a conviction.

The most obvious hypothesis that comes to mind is that Ann Melton killed Laura Foster. Whether she actually did or not is of little consequence to the point being made. The point is that she could have, and this alone is sufficient to raise reasonable doubt that Tom Dula did.

Another reasonable hypothesis which comes to mind is that anyone, known or unknown, within the general neighborhood could have perpetrated the crime, including the witnesses themselves who saw Tom Dula in the general area.

Most certainly Tom Dula could have had a valid reason and explanation for his actions and conduct on or about the time that Laura Foster disappeared other than the act of committing murder. He lived in the general area himself, he frequently passed back and forth on the road on which he was seen. There could have been many reasons why he had a mattock in his hands, including the one which is implied by the cross-examination of his lawyer − that is, that he was skelping the road. Even his conduct in leaving the country is subject to the reasonable conclusion that he wanted to get out of a situation where people were accusing him of such a crime, that the suspicions of the neighborhood made him uncomfortable, or even that he knew Ann Melton or some other party had committed the crime and wanted to protect them from whatever knowledge he had.

If the reader desires to compare further the standards of proof required by the present Supreme Court of North Carolina to convict one of crime upon circumstantial evidence alone, he should read the case of State vs. Holland, 234 NC 354; State v. Hendrick, 232 NC 447; and State vs. Coffey, 28 NC 119.

After reviewing this record, I can only conclude that if the Tom Dula case arose today and the evidence admitted against him was identical to the evidence presented in the record of this case, there seems little question but that his conviction at this second trial would have been set aside because of insufficient evidence. Since there was apparently no further direct evidence linking him with the commission of the crime, it seems most likely that he would ultimately have gone free. Apparently the folklore I heard as a child had some substance to it.

BIBLIOGRAPHY

Ashe, Samuel A., Editor. BIOGRAPHICAL HISTORY OF NORTH CAROLINA. 8 volumes. Greensboro, 1907.

Brown, Frank C., Editor. NORTH CAROLINA FOLKLORE. II & IV. Durham, North Carolina: Duke University Press, 1952.

Dawd, Clement. LIFE OF ZEBULON B. VANCE. Charlotte, North Carolina, 1897.

Greensboro *Daily News*, February 1, 1959.

Greensboro *Daily News* February 8, 1959.

Hayes, Johnson J. THE LAND OF WILKES. North Wilkesboro, North Carolina: Wilkes County Historical Society, 1962.

Henry, Mellinger Edward, Editor. FOLK-SONGS FROM THE SOUTHERN HIGHLANDS. New York: J. J. Augustin, 1938.

Hickerson, Thomas Felix. HAPPY VALLEY. Chapel Hill, North Carolina: (published by author), 1940.

Hickerson, Thomas Felix. ECHOES OF HAPPY VALLEY. Chapel Hill, North Carolina: (published by author), 1962.

Isbell, Robert L. THE WORLD OF MY CHILDHOOD. Lenoir, North Carolina: The Lenoir *News Topic*, 1955.

NORTH CAROLINA REPORTS, Volume 61, June Term, 1866 to January Term, 1868; annotated.

Tucker, Glenn. ZEB VANCE. New York: The Bobbs-Merrill Co., 1965.

Warner, Frank. "Frank Profitt." SING OUT (October-November, 1963). p. 10.

Wellman, Manly Wade. DEAD AND GONE. Chapel Hill, North Carolina: University of North Carolina Press, 1954.

Winston-Salem *Journal*, November 17. 1958.